D0728527

The Preschool Resource Guide

Educating and Entertaining Children Aged Two through Five

Property of the Library
YORK COUNTY TECHNICAL COLLEGE
112 College Dr.
Wells, Maine 04090
(207) 646-9282

The Preschool Resource Guide

Educating and Entertaining Children Aged Two through Five

Harriet Friedes, M.A.

Introduction by
Beatrice Teitel, Ph.D.

INSIGHT BOOKS

Plenum Press • New York and London

Library of Congress Cataloging-in-Publication Data

Friedes, Harriet.
    The preschool resource guide : educating and entertaining children
aged two through five / Harriet Friedes ; introduction by Beatrice
Teitel.
        p.   cm.
    "Insight books."
    Includes bibliographical references and index.
    ISBN 0-306-44464-X. -- ISBN 0-306-44473-9 (pbk.)
    1. Preschool children--Bibliography. 2. Preschool children--Audio
-visual aids. 3. Preschool children--Information services.
    4. Child rearing--Bibliography. I. Title.
    Z7164.C5F76   1993
    [HQ774.5]
    016.30523'3--dc20   92-41250
                                                          CIP

Property of the Library
YORK COUNTY TECHNICAL COL
112 College Dr.
Wells, Maine 040
(207) 646-92

10 9 8 7 6 5 4 3 2

Illustrations by Kevin Atkinson

ISBN 0-306-44464-X (Hardbound)
ISBN 0-306-44473-9 (Paperback)

© 1993 Plenum Press, New York
A Division of Plenum Publishing Corporation
233 Spring Street, New York, N.Y. 10013

An Insight Book

All rights reserved

No part of this book may be reproduced, stored in a retrieval system, or transmitted
in any form or by any means, electronic, mechanical, photocopying, microfilming,
recording, or otherwise, without written permission from the Publisher

Printed in the United States of America

Preface

"What is a good, safe toy for my 2-year-old granddaughter?"
"My 3-year-old likes dogs. What book do you suggest?"
"Should I buy a computer for my 5-year-old?"

The Preschool Resource Guide is intended to answer questions such as these, and to help parents, teachers, caregivers, librarians, and others provide the very best for their young children. The guide identifies and describes the highest-rated books, magazines, toys, software, audios, and videos specifically geared to children aged 2 through 5 and presents information, advice, and support for parents and professionals. Individual chapters have been designed as self-contained units, so that either the book can be read in its entirety or particular parts can be consulted as needed.

I have taken great care to try to make this reference as comprehensive and authoritative as possible. Each item selected for inclusion is based upon recommendations of leading experts, and apologies are made in advance for the fine works that have necessarily been omitted. Product availability, prices, and other specifics are accurate at the time of printing but are frequently subject to change. I would very much appreciate receiving reader feedback, comments, and suggestions; please send these to Insight Books, 233 Spring Street, New York, New York 10013-1578.

Acknowledgments

I am extremely grateful to the many wonderful people who gave so generously of their time and expertise in the preparation of this book. Unfortunately, I cannot acknowledge them all by name but especially want to thank the following (in alphabetical order): Warren Buckleitner, High/Scope Educational Research Foundation; Peggy Charren, Action for Children's Television; Barbara Elleman, Book Links Magazine, American Library Association; Donna Fox, Eastman School of Music; Ruth Flynn, Director of Early Childhood Education, Missouri Department of Education; Marilyn Kay, The Reading Group; Pat Lutzky, Educational Products Information Exchange (EPIE Institute); Joanne Oppenheim, Bank Street College of Education; Janet Peterson, World Book Encyclopedia; Elizabeth F. Shores, Southern Early Childhood Association (SECA); Mary Ann Smith, Eastman School of Music; Ella Wilcox, Music Educators National Conference. On a more personal level, I am indebted to Rona Distenfeld, for "showing me the way," and Helen Bloch, both expert book reviewers and helpmates; Ellen Sternhell for her indispensable ideas and insights; Larry Abrams for his valued friendship and support; and my father and sister for their never-failing reassurance and love. Heartfelt thanks go to Dr. Beatrice Teitel for her advice and encouragement throughout and without whom this book would never have been written, and, most especially, to dear Ariel, for his steadfast patience, wisdom, and caring.

Grateful acknowledgment is also made to the following for permission to reprint previously published material:

Missouri Department of Elementary and Secondary Education: Excerpts from *How Does Your Child Grow and Learn?* Copyright 1982. Reprinted 1988. Used with permission.

Reading Is Fundamental, Inc.: Excerpts from *Magazines and Family Reading*. Copyright 1988 by Reading Is Fundamental, Inc. All rights reserved. Reprinted with permission.

World Book Publishing: "105 Desirable Readiness Skills." Excerpted from *Getting Ready for School*. Copyright 1987 World Book, Inc. By permission of the publisher.

Contents

Introduction

by Beatrice Teitel, Ph.D.

Alex crept over to the coffee table and reached for the book *Goodnight Moon*. He knocked it to the floor and pushed it over to where his mother, Beth, was sitting on the couch, and he made noises until she picked up the book. She also picked up Alex from the floor and settled him in her lap. Alex quieted down and watched the pages being turned and listened to the rhythmic words he had heard many times before. He wiggles with pleasure. How old was Alex? Not quite a year. Did he understand all the words that were being read? Could he connect the words with the pictures? Unlikely. But he did know that something special was happening that was giving him a good feeling. He was learning to associate a book with pleasure, and had possibly taken the first important step toward becoming a lifetime reader.

This classic book by Margaret Wise Brown was introduced to Alex as a bedtime story when he was 4 months old. It is by far his favorite; he has asked his parents to reread the story many times. Now Alex is 5 and he still sometimes asks for *Goodnight Moon*. Although he now frequently shares reading the book with an adult, he also spends time alone with the book, engaging in what is known as "reading-like behavior." The words he says may not be the exact text, but the meaning is clear. Through his many experiences with books, he has learned the conventions of print—that the words come from the squiggly letters, not from the illustrations, that reading begins from the front of the book and progresses to the back, and that the eye moves in a left-to-right direction, from the top to the bottom. These are the first steps to early literacy.

When we think about it, what is it that we want for our children? We want them to grow up to be responsible, caring, competent people. We want them to feel good about themselves and to be risk takers—not fearful of trying something new along the road of growing up. We want them to learn to read and write and think, and to *want* to do all these things. How do these strengths come about? What role do we as parents play in this process?

Part of the answer is provided by an important study that dates back to the 1960s which suggests that children who enter kindergarten already reading have certain commonalities in their backgrounds that cut across racial, socioeconomic lines.[1] These children had someone who read to them on a regular basis—a parent, caregiver, or sibling (the children were also known as paper-and-pencil kids, who loved to write marks on paper). In addition, someone was available to answer their questions, so they remained curious, and they lived in a print-rich environment. They saw people reading and writing, leaving notes on the refrigerator, consulting a cookbook for a recipe. Let's keep this in mind as we explore some findings of a more recent researcher.

A leader in current thinking regarding language learning, Brian Cambourne of the University of Wollongong in Australia proposes that there are several conditions that should be present when children are learning oral language, that is, how to talk.[2] Learning to talk is a most impressive feat. Those of us who, as adults, have tried to learn another language are aware of the complexities. Yet very young children learn the language of the culture into which they are born and have been doing so for thousands of years.

Cambourne believes that in order to learn how to talk, one must be human, and certain other conditions must operate to permit language to occur. Furthermore, he asserts that these conditions are relevant to other areas of language learning—reading and writing. It is generally believed that children will learn to talk quite naturally, but it is assumed that learning to read and write are very complicated tasks and need special teaching—that the written form of language is so very different from the oral one. Reasearch shows that children will learn to read and write with the same ease with which they learn to talk, if the same conditions prevail. Let's look at some of the conditions put forth by Cambourne and explore what parents can do in the early years to help meet the conditions, and at the same time, determine if there is such a sharp line of demarcation between oral and written language.

Immersion is Cambourne's first condition for learning language. Children who are surrounded by talk will learn to talk more readily than those who live in silent surroundings. Many opportunities are present in the very early years when the infant needs much physical care. For example, when the child is being bathed, fed, dressed, or comforted, the caregiver may accompany the actions with words like, "Now we have to get under the fat chin to wash," or "In a minute we'll have lunch ready," or "We have to find the other sock to put on your other foot," or "Let me hold you, so you can burp." The child may be far too young to understand the actual words, but he does begin to associate the words with a subsequent action that meets his needs or makes him feel better. Put another way, the language is functional, and it lays the groundwork for the idea that needs can be met by using words.

When we talk with a child, we help build a richer knowledge of vocabulary, sentence structure, and language usage. We can talk about what the child has been doing, what we have been doing, what is going on in the world, on the block, in school, in the house. When is the right time? Mealtimes, bathtime, bedtime, in a car or bus, after watching a good TV program together, after a visit or family experience—these are all natural times that talk occurs. Of course, interchange of ideas is not limited to these times and should be encouraged anytime. We certainly would not confine talking to three 15-minute segments a day.

Let's extend talk a bit to the print that surrounds us. We, as adults, can become aware of our print-rich environment and use it to teach our children language. When faced with two doors leading to bathrooms, mother takes the child through the door that says "Ladies" and comments on the meaning of the word while pointing to the sign. The same applies when looking at a recipe on a box, or at directions on how to assemble a toy. If the caregiver prefaces the reading with a statement to the effect that we need to read the words in order to know what to do, the child soon learns that there is a purpose in reading. Imagine parking on a street without careful examination of the signs that indicate the days and hours that parking is legal. The car may not be there when we come back! The familiar McDonald's logo is probably one of the first signs young children recognize (as well as *keep off the grass* and *up/down* if they live in a high-rise building). Again, language (this time print) serves a function—to tell us something that informs or helps us.

Is there print in the home? Are books, magazines, and newspapers in evidence? When we go shopping, do we look at the ads for specials? How do we check out a favorite program on TV? Are clothes or products ever ordered from a mail-order catalogue? Is the telephone directory used to locate a phone number? A bus or train schedule will tell us how to organize our time so we can get to the station on time. When my children were young, I would carry my print with me—a couple of books, tucked in my bag—so when the checkout line was long, or there was a wait at the dentist's office, reading a story helped to make the wait more pleasurable, and often was a calming influence when the children became restless. In a New Zealand bank I observed children reading interesting books taken from a pile on the table while their parent conducted business with a teller.

What kinds of books should be read to children? Certainly books that they like—and that the adult likes too, because the re-reading may be very frequent. For advice about books to meet the interest of children, the librarian in the children's section is an excellent resource for titles appropriate to various age levels. Additional sources will be mentioned in the chapter about books for preschool children. I found that predictable books—those that are highly patterned so children anticipate what is going to happen—scored high in my family. They ranged from alphabet books, to counting books, to books with repeated wording, like *The Little Red Hen,* or with repeated grammatical patterns, like *Chicken Soup with Rice,* where the format and rhythm are the same, but different words are substituted. *Brown Bear, Brown Bear, What Do You See?* is a fine example of a predictable book with link wording—the last word of one phrase becomes the first word of the next. A book with cumulative structure is one in which an episode is repeated and a new one added. *I Know an Old Lady Who Swallowed a Fly* is a representative example. A book like *The Very Hungry Caterpillar* illustrates concept development—in this case, the days of the week and the numerals 1 through 7 are presented. Rhyming books are favorites, too. And wordless books that have pictures that tell a story are great for children who wish to create their own text. *A Boy, a Dog and a Frog* is one of many in this genre. We must not forget nursery rhymes, which children love because of the rhythm, which makes it impossible to chant without tapping a toe or a finger. Using predictable books invites children to chime in and quickly take over the reading.

Just as a print-rich environment contributes to the belief that adults place a value on reading, we could extend that concept to writing. Are there materials available that make it easier for youngsters to "make the marks" on paper? I have found that putting special items for writing in one place is helpful. Included could be paper, markers, scissors, paste, scotch tape, old magazines, pictures. These may be assembled in a shallow carton or a bureau drawer. In this way, while an adult is involved with a chore around the house, the child can be writing, taking the tray or drawer to wherever the adult is. Again, the presence of this equipment indicates a value placed on writing.

Demonstration, or modeling, is the second condition for learning language. When a parent asks a child to "Please get me the small paperback book that is on the white table next to the red lamp," the parent is demonstrating the richness and clarity of language. How different that statement is from pointing to an object and saying, "Get me that." Similarly, the parent does not accept a finger-pointing request from the child. It might be better to close eyes and say, "I can't see. You have to tell me what you want by using words." It works.

When you are a model for reading, your children will see you read in a variety of situations, using different materials for different reasons—cookbooks, instructional materials, road signs, maps, informational books (dictionaries, encyclopedias), magazines. The old adage "Do as I Say, Not as I Do" is certainly relevant here. If children see their parents watch TV after dinner, yet advise their offspring to get a book to read, it's a rather mixed message. But should the adults turn off the TV, unplug the telephone, take out reading material, and declare it a family reading time, the message is clear—"We value reading and invite you to join us in this activity."

If an adult is writing a thank-you note or an invitation to a party, children are seeing some of the reasons for writing. Sometimes the parent leaves space at the bottom of the letter so the child may add her own personal message—a scrawl or a picture will do. Early on, when the parent is sending a birthday or holiday greeting card, the child may again join in and create his own. There may be a large family calendar, and important events are written in—dental appointments, an arranged visit with a friend or a relative, a birthday party. A bulletin board may be set up in the kitchen on which samples of the children's work are displayed. Magnetic letters may be attached to the refrigerator with which children can make words, usually starting with their names. It is important that parents are accepting of early writing attempts. Show through reactions that what your child produces is valued.

Approximation and feedback are the next conditions offered by Cambourne. Early efforts to walk are accepted and celebrated. In the beginning, the baby falls, gets up, takes some tentative steps, falls again, and keeps trying. We encourage the attempts. The same is true with talking. When the babbling is suddenly recognized as the word "mama" or "dada," there is great joy. A fuss is made, and the child repeats the word—again and again—to the same warm acceptance. When my granddaughter Kate calls "Bamaw" when I ring the doorbell, do I walk in and say, "That's not the way we say it. Repeat after me, g-r-and-mo-ther"? Of course not. I celebrate the attempts and say, "Yes, grandma is here." The feedback is positive. Yet, when it comes to early efforts at reading and writing, we expect perfection at the start. We often don't celebrate that the child has retained the meaning of a selection by substituting dad for father, but are concerned that the child is not using phonics to figure out the word. We worry that early struggles with writing may produce text that is not spelled perfectly or is messy. The message we give is that we expect expertness, and anything short of that is not acceptable. The feedback is not positive. The child may react by not taking risks. If she is not absolutely sure of the reading material, she may refuse to even try. If there is uncertainty about spelling a word, the tendency would be to write the word that is known to be correct. This often leads to stilted, unimaginative text that is "safe." The curiosity and risk-taking have been stilled. However, with a little bit of practice, a parent would soon be able to translate W S A P N A T M as "once upon a time."

This concern for perfection is reflected in the attitudes adults have about writing. Every year when I meet with my graduate students I ask how many of them write—not reports or shopping lists—but letters or journals. The response is predictable. Very few write, and the reasons given are generally uncertainty about spelling, poor handwriting, unsureness about punctuation—the same concerns they had as children just learning to put marks on paper. We have to be aware that just as it took time to learn how to walk without falling, and to talk to be understood, it will take time to write competently. But a parent's reaction and feedback to early efforts will matter a great deal. Be uncritical in the early attempts. Show through your reactions that you value your child and what the child produced.

Expectation is another condition Cambourne offers. Our expectations are that our children will learn to walk and talk. Somehow, we communicate these expectations to them. Learning to walk can be a slow, possibly painful experience, and learning to talk can be a complicated, frustrating task, but unless there is some severe damage, they learn. However, many parents give off the expectation that learning to read, write, and spell is complex and possibly beyond the children's abilities. Perhaps a sibling or one of the parents had trouble learning these skills, and these concerned expectations are picked up by the children, who then may respond accordingly. It is, therefore, important that we maintain a relaxed expectation and this feeling will be communicated to and give children the confidence needed to take risks.

Employment is Cambourne's final condition. When our children learned to walk and talk, we provided them with many opportunities to do so. They practiced relentlessly, and with practice, they became more proficient and enjoyed the experiences more and more. Reading and writing, too, improve with practice. Parents sometimes have to create situations and schedule time for children to use their new skills, if other activities fill the day so they don't have a chance to get the practice they need to become more proficient. Here, too, enjoyment of books is accelerated by the ease they experience in reading them. Picture and story books are not the only kinds of books they should be exposed to. Poetry, folktales, fantasy, and nonfiction books will expand and broaden their world. And they will be able to learn, and experience pleasure.

Beth and her husband, Bill, are wonderful parents who recognize their important role as Alex's first teachers, nurturing his needs and recognizing his interests. They want to do the very best for Alex, and they can make his life even richer if they are aware of the resources available to them outside the home. Like many young parents, they need to know which materials have been evaluated and designated as having met high standards of excellence. This book introduces them to children's books, magazines, records, videos, computer software, toys, and games that have met this test.

It is hoped that a continuing understanding of the importance of the role of parents, the awareness of conditions that lead to language learning, and the excellent resources available outside the home will contribute to better-informed parents, better-informed children, and better relationships between the two.

Prologue

The Preschool Child

To observe and be part of the blossoming of a toddler of 2 into a kindergarten kid of 5 is an amazing experience. The years between the two ages are a time of rapid growth; a period marked by many wondrous physical, mental, and emotional changes. It is natural for parents to wonder whether their children are developing "normally" and how they compare with other youngsters of the same age.

Experts in the field of child development have found that although maturation follows an orderly pattern, there is a wide range of individual differences among children. Especially during the early years, a child's growth is frequently uneven, with some areas surging ahead and others lagging behind. More important than a timetable for acquiring skills is that children progress and learn at a comfortable pace in a pressure-free environment.

Even with the recognition of individual variations, however, there are certain "signposts" that have been identified for specific age groups. The following characteristics, behaviors, and skills for ages 2 through 5 with suggestions for adult involvement[1] are intended as general guidelines and must not be considered absolute measures of success or failure. It is important to keep in mind that every child is unique. What may not show up today may burst forth tomorrow.

SIGNPOSTS FOR AGE 2

Anyone who has spent time with a 2-year-old can attest to surprising and delightful experiences as well as exhausting and

Age 2: Growth and Development

Large and Small Body Movements	Language and Thinking Skills	Self-Awareness and Self-Care
• Balances on one foot alone. • Jumps with both feet. • Pedals a tricycle. • Responds to music by swaying and bending. • Turns handles to make objects move. • Fills and dumps containers of sand or water. • Builds a tower of five to eight blocks. • Rolls, pounds, squeezes, pulls clay. • Cuts with blunt scissors. • Copies a circle.	• Enjoys simple stories read from picture books. • Joins in songs and nursery rhymes. • Says a few nursery rhymes. • Uses vocabulary of 50–500 words. • Constantly asks names of objects. • Begins to use pronouns, such as "mine," "me," "you," and "I." • Asks questions in sentences. • Uses plurals of words. • Repeats two numbers. • Understands prepositions, such as "on," "under," and "in."	• Gives full name when asked. • Refers to self by name. • Points to six to eight body parts on request. • Knows own sex. • Spoon-feeds without spilling. • Gets a drink without help. • Dries hands without help. • Helps put things away. • Plays near but not with others. • Usually maintains bladder and bowel control, except for fatigue, illness, excitement, or preoccupation.

frustrating ones. On the surprising, delightful side is the child's beginning ability to coordinate large and small body movements in purposeful ways, to use language for expressing needs and wants, and to develop thought processes for anticipating and solving problems. On the exhausting and frustrating side are some of the very same characteristics—along with a newly discovered power of saying "No!" to suggestions, requests, or commands from adults.

So how does one cope with a 2-year-old's asking to hear music, stories, and poems again and again, holding real and imaginary conversations, trying to help with feeding and dressing, actively exploring, touching (even breaking) things—and saying "No"? With appreciation, understanding, guidance, and patience. The child of 2 is truly just beginning to realize that there is a world to fit into, master, and enjoy. All the experiences—even the "No's"—are part of the child's process of learning who she is and what she can do. It is a part of the changing from a dependent toddler to an independent, whole human being.

Age 2: How Parents/Caregivers Can Help

- Tell and retell favorite poems, nursery rhymes, and short stories with and without picture books; encourage reciting of familiar parts and adding original ideas.
- Foster good language by taking lead from child's interests, responding to questions, and adding to information. Be a good role model; use full sentences, rich, descriptive language, and substitute words for "pointing."
- Arrange play experiences with small groups of children where opportunities to be a leader or a follower will develop naturally.

- Make available "props" for make-believe play, such as large cardboard cartons for stoves, store counters, or buses, and dress-up materials, such as shoes, hats, and purses.
- Provide a variety of materials for creative expression, including finger paints, play dough, and large crayons. Allow use of blunt scissors.
- Share musical experiences through singing, listening, and playing instruments.
- Encourage noting likenesses, differences, and details in toys and pictures by asking questions and adding comments.
- Praise accomplishments and mastery of new skills.
- Accept expressions of affection and of displeasure as a natural part of growing up; hostile behavior or temper tantrums need understanding, consistency, limits, avoidance of power struggles, and, if possible, a sense of humor.

SIGNPOSTS FOR AGE 3

Ah, the 3-year-old! After having just spent a year testing everything and exhausting everyone, a 3-year-old moves into a period of enlightenment that includes a miraculous desire to please adults (thank goodness). Thus this stage of exploration and discovery is an enjoyable experience for all concerned!

Enlightenment for a child of 3 takes many forms: realizing that there is a world outside the home environment and feeling confident enough to want to be part of it; discovering control of bodily functions and how to attend to personal care needs; learning more about language and the power of words. With the ever-increasing agility of the body and abilities of the mind, the 3-year-old spends more time on tasks that require fine muscle

Age 3: Growth and Development

Large and Small Body Movements	Language and Thinking Skills	Self-Awareness and Self-Care
• Walks heel to toe.	• Has vocabulary of 500– 1500 words.	• Refers to self as "I" or "me."
• Kicks a ball well.	• Uses names of things and action words.	• Performs for others.
• Catches a large bounced ball.	• Whispers.	• Talks to self while playing.
• Sits with feet crossed at the ankles.	• Repeats six-word sentences.	• Joins in play with other children.
• Closes fists, wiggles thumbs.	• Tells a story from a picture.	• Understands sharing playthings.
• Builds with blocks.	• Recites a poem or sings a song from memory.	• Makes effort to keep surroundings tidy
• Strings large wooden beads.	• Names hidden objects from memory.	• Cares for toileting needs.
• Holds a crayon with fingers.	• Acts out simple stories.	• Separates from mother easily.
• Copies vertical and horizontal lines, and a cross if shown how.	• Answers questions using comparatives, such as bigger, heavier, smaller.	• Likes to help with adult activities.
• Attempts to draw a person.	• Shows some awareness of past and present.	• Shows affection for younger sister or brother.

control and coordination; enjoys being with other children; and begins to converse, count, question, compare, and differentiate.

Age 3: How Parents/Caregivers Can Help

- Provide opportunities for child to practice new motor skills of jumping, kicking, and catching.
- Set good language patterns by using complete sentences with vocabulary aimed at or a little above child's level of understanding.

- Spend time in "private" conversation when youngster does not have to compete with other family members or activities for undivided attention. Listen attentively and actively.
- Continue to arrange small play group experiences for learning how to take turns and play cooperatively.
- Visit interesting places where child can learn firsthand about other people, animals, and things.
- Continue to provide a variety of art activities. Occasionally provide simple patterns which can be copied, or from which original designs can be created.
- Show child how things that are alike in some way may be grouped together, such as food, clothing, or animals. Have child sort laundry, match socks, or use pictures from magazines or catalogs.
- Take advantage of times when child wants to help around the house to discover concepts of bigger, heavier, lighter, warmer, etc.
- Help child anticipate what comes next or what to expect, by alerting a few minutes beforehand to wash for meals, watch for the mail, or get ready for a favorite TV program.

SIGNPOSTS FOR AGE 4

Variety and complexity—are they part of a 4-year-old's world? They are. A child of 4 thrives on trying many new things and is developing the staying power to handle more difficult tasks for longer periods of time. What keeps the child interested is an expanding curiosity about the world and how it works, an increasing sense of pride in accomplishments, and an exploding imagination.

While physical growth enables a 4-year-old to focus on

Age 4: Growth and Development

Large and Small Body Movements	Language and Thinking Skills	Self-Awareness and Self-Care
• Balances 10 seconds on one foot.	• Has vocabulary of 1,500–2,000 words.	• Brags or boasts.
• Walks downstairs, alternating feet.	• Repeats eight- to ten-word sentences.	• May have an imaginary playmate.
• Throws a ball overhand with direction.	• Uses five- to six-word sentences.	• Tells age in whole years.
• Catches a small bounced ball.	• Recites songs and poems from memory.	• Gives address correctly.
• Laces shoes, buttons clothing.	• Speaks clearly enough for a stranger to understand.	• Shows pride in accomplishment.
• Draws a very simple house.	• Asks "Why?" "When?" "How?" frequently.	• Washes face and hands without help.
• Adds parts to an incomplete drawing of a person.	• Names four to eight basic colors.	• Offers to help with chores.
• Copies a square.	• Counts four objects and tells how many.	• Knows the names of other children and adults.
• Prints letters and simple words.	• Names three common coins.	• Stands up for his or her own rights.
• Prints first name.	• Relates seasons to events.	• Plays competitive exercise games, such as "Tag" and "Hide and Seek."

activities that require more complex motor coordination skills, it is in language and thinking skills that great changes are even more apparent. The wonderful bundle of energy is becoming aware of time concepts (yesterday, today, tomorrow), recognizing the difference between "real" and "pretend," developing a sense of humor, starting to print letters and draw specific things (most of the time unrecognizable to everyone but the child), and perhaps even trying to be bossy. In short, the 4-year-old is reaching out to connect, communicate, and control!

Age 4: How Parents/Caregivers Can Help

- Teach child his or her full name and address. Knowing telephone number and parents' names are also important as a safeguard in case child gets lost.
- Arrange occasions for using large muscles for running, jumping, catching, and playing on playground equipment.
- Encourage child to dress independently by providing clothing that can be handled.
- Provide opportunities to develop school readiness behaviors of following simple directions and listening when others are talking.
- Share simple poems and songs, and encourage child to learn favorites by heart.
- Stimulate interest in letters and words that are seen regularly, as on food labels, street signs, in books, and in child's own name.
- Encourage interest in paper-and-crayon activities. Show child how his or her name looks when printed; praise attempts to copy and write from memory.
- Introduce numbers and number concepts in meaningful ways, such as counting out spoons for the table, noticing numbers on people's houses, and noting when the hands of the clock say it's supper time.
- Play simple card and board games, such as "Animal Rummy, " checkers, and dominoes, which involve counting, matching, and concentrating.

SIGNPOSTS FOR AGE 5

One might think that the energy exerted during the fourth year of life might be used up. Not so. A child of 5 continues to have boundless energy for both physical and mental activities. In addition to running and jumping and hopping and climbing, a 5-year-old is also tying bows, sewing, measuring, matching, pouring, squeezing, drawing, writing, perhaps reading, and talk-

Age 5: Growth and Development

Large and Small Body Movements	Language and Thinking Skills	Self-Awareness and Self Care
• Skips using alternate feet.	• Has vocabulary of 5,000 words.	• Knows family name, telephone number, and birthday.
• Throws and kicks simultaneously.	• Speaks in compound and complex sentences.	• Is relatively independent and self-reliant.
• Cuts with scissors.		
• Threads a needle with a large eye.	• Names the days of the week in sequence.	
• Grasps a pencil correctly.	• Counts to 20.	• Is polite and courteous.
• Traces accurately.	• Repeats five numbers.	• Separates easily from home.
• Colors within a boundary.	• Identifies shapes of circle, square, triangle, and rectangle.	• Enjoys friendships and group activities.
• Copies a triangle.	• Categorizes objects by color, size, and shape.	• Completes tasks.
• Prints upper- and lower-case letters.		• Seeks approval and affection from others.
• Writes numbers through 10.	• Differentiates between reality and fantasy.	• Understands and feels compassion for others.
	• Recognizes words by sight.	• Develops a social conscience.
	• Identifies letter sounds.	

ing, talking, talking. At this age, however, the child does not particularly like to listen to other children.[2]

As dominant as the level of energy is at age 5, so too is the level of concentration for extended periods of time. A 5-year-old is eager to learn and now willingly puts in the time to this end. Thus the manipulating of materials, the "reading" of books, the dramatizing, the creating, the experimenting, the socializing all have a more focused purpose. And along with a sense of purpose is a strong self-pride about work well done. The 5-year-old has come a long way!

Age 5: How Parents/Caregivers Can Help

- Encourage child to think and talk about experiences. Focus on past and future events, as well as present ones, to help child reflect, use memories, and tell complete stories.
- Read aloud; improve comprehension by having child summarize story, sequence events, and answer thought-provoking questions relating to the plot, characters, and illustrations.
- Play traveling games with road signs, maps, and license plates. Encourage child to identify symbols, letters, words, and numbers.[3]
- Share with child articles and books about favorite sports, movies, and singing stars.[4]
- Provide writing materials, such as paper, pencils, crayons, chalk, and magnetic boards and letters.
- Encourage problem-solving and estimating skills with such questions as "Which dish will hold all the potatoes?" or "Do we have enough milk for dinner?"
- Limit television to 10 hours a week. Monitor and share viewing if possible.

- Set a good example by frequent reading and writing and attending to and completing adult responsibilities.
- Arrange a place where child can play and work quietly, preferably with good lighting and few distractions.[5]
- Encourage self-confidence by acknowledging and praising skills and accomplishments.

Part I

THE BEST RESOURCES FOR PRESCHOOL CHILDREN

KEVIN ATKINSON

Chapter 1

Audio Recordings

KEVIN ATKINSON

The allure and appeal of audios have long been appreciated by children, parents, and educators, but now the music industry is catching on too. Cited as a "hot" area for growth, it's being called quality entertainment for kids that doesn't involve being glued to the TV.[1]

Audios have many other advantages. They can liven up play groups, be the inspiration for shared parent–child activities, create harmony on long trips, extend appreciation of storybooks,[2] and provide often needed "quiet times." They promote listening proficiency in today's video-dominated society, and they stimulate children to learn, sing, play, imagine, laugh, and grow emotionally and intellectually![3]

MAGIC OF MUSIC

Recordings are also a marvelous medium for music during the formative preschool years. Music is a natural motivator of movement, and whether swinging, swaying, tapping, or clapping, children practice motor and coordination skills. When listening to songs and sounds, youngsters build concepts and language; while singing or dancing with others, they develop social and group awareness. Music is a way to celebrate heritage, transmit traditions, and connect cultures. Music can spur self-expression, soothe and satisfy, and provide pleasure throughout life!

MUSIC MILESTONES

The following guidelines provide a general picture of the progression of musical skills in children aged 2 through 5. It is important to remember, though, that these milestones will vary depending on each individual child's rate and level of maturation.

Age 2

- Sings, hums, chants at play.
- Begins to sing phrases or short songs, although not on pitch.
- Likes songs with repetition.
- Prefers music with a strong beat and a definite pattern.
- Moves body to music by rocking, swaying, swinging, bouncing, though not always in rhythm.
- Loves to hear favorites repeated again and again.

Age 3

- Recognizes and imitates simple melodies.
- Sings phrases and songs with increasing accuracy.
- Creates own tunes.
- Begins to participate in group singing.
- Learns some singing games, such as "Ring around the Rosy."
- Moves body more in rhythm to the music.
- Begins to form concepts of loud and soft, fast and slow.

Age 4

- Sings with increased voice control and pitch accuracy.
- Expands vocal range.

- Enjoys group singing and games.
- Likes silly songs, action songs, songs relating to familiar experiences, and songs that can be dramatized.
- Synchronizes movements to music; begins to use smaller body parts, such as hand clapping.
- Plays most rhythm instruments.
- Increases listening attention span.

Age 5

- Sings with greater accuracy with regard to pitch, tone, loudness.
- Improvises with increased experimentation and sophistication.
- Enjoys silly songs, echo songs, answer-back songs.
- Maintains beat when moving to music and playing instruments.
- Expands attention span when listening to recordings.

AUDIO ADVICE

The suggestions that follow motivate music appreciation and abilities:

- Incorporate music into the daily routine. Parents can invent "personalized" ditties to accompany chores and activities,[4] and use music as a backdrop for playing and eating.
- Focus on music. Children can listen to music on radio and tapes, watch musical programs on television, and, if possible, attend children's concerts where the programs will be more appropriate, varied, and movement-oriented than adult performances.

- Encourage responsiveness. Reacting to music with movement, dance, instruments, and dramatization should be nurtured. Drawing attention to the rhythm and lyrics, sharing feelings, and using props, such as scarves, hats, yarn, and beanbags, enhance enjoyment and experimentation.
- Provide variety. Preschool children are generally open to all kinds of music, and they should be introduced to many differing styles, such as contemporary, classical, folk, rock, and jazz.
- Start a collection. A few very-own favorites can go a long way toward stimulating a preschooler's interest in and love for music. A sturdy, easy-to-operate children's cassette player is recommended for independence in choosing and playing selections.
- Call attention to sounds. Games can be played in which children listen, identify, imitate, compare, and categorize various sounds in the home and neighborhood.
- Be sensitive and available. Youngsters need approval for their musical efforts, and adult involvement adds to everyone's fun.

A GUIDE TO THE BEST

The explosive growth in children's music offers an accelerating acoustical menu. To assist parents and caregivers in choosing the best, the following top-rated titles for preschool-age children are provided (see "References" for specific sources). They represent a variety of material and styles, as well as a mix of old standards and newer releases. They concentrate on musical selections; the chapter on preschool books should be consulted for the very best titles in recorded literature. For convenience in locating a particular type of recording, titles have been grouped into four main categories—Song Standards, Play Songs/Quiet Songs, Fun and Learning, and Popular Favorites—although diverse preschool tapes often fit into more than one classification. Other recommended recordings by the same artist are included in the "Comments" section. Each entry contains the title, targeted age, recording format and length, publication date, price, producer/distributor, description, and comments.

It should be noted that parents need not feel compelled to restrict musical experiences to children's recordings alone. Sharing enthusiasm and love for special adult favorites is not only acceptable but advised.

Song Standards

Activity and Game Songs for Children (Volumes 1 and 2) (Ages 2–4, LP, Cassette, $9.95, 1973, 36 minutes; Alcazar, P.O. Box 429, Waterbury, VT 05676, 800-541-9904)

DESCRIPTION: A super sing-along with Tom Glazer and hundreds of kids as they perform all the old favorites with energy and enthusiasm. Includes such standards as "This Old Man," "Skip to My Lou," and Tom's original, "On Top of Spaghetti."

COMMENTS: Others by Tom: *Children's Greatest Hits, Let's Sing Fingerplays,* and for toddlers: *Music for Ones and Twos, More Music for Ones and Twos.*

Francine Sings a Keepsake of Mother Goose and Other Nursery Songs (Ages 1–5, Cassette/Songbook, $16.95; Cassette only, $9.95, 1987, 38 minutes; Lancaster Productions, P.O. Box 7820, Berkeley, CA 94707-0820, 415-652-3228)

DESCRIPTION: The beautiful soprano voice of Francine Lancaster and members of the San Francisco Boys and Girls

Chorus present more than 20 well-known rhymes and songs. The cassette is accompanied by a superb songbook, produced jointly with Boston's Museum of Fine Arts, with Victorian reproductions, lyrics, and scores.

COMMENTS: Other Lancaster Keepsake recordings: *Favorite Animal Songs, Favorite Holiday Songs,* and *Nursery Songs and Lullabies.*

If You're Happy and You Know It, Sing with Bob (Volumes 1 and 2) (2–5, LP, Cassette, $9.94 each, 1985, 45 minutes each; Educational Record Center, 1575 Northside Drive, N.W., Atlanta, GA 30318-4298, 800-438-1637)

DESCRIPTION: Bob McGrath of Sesame Street puts everyone in high humor with this very complete collection of almost 70 standards that have been a mainstay of nursery school and day-care centers for years.

COMMENTS: *Songs and Games for Toddlers* (1½–3), with Katharine Smithrim, promotes parent–child participation.

Jump Children (2–6, Disc, Cassette, $8.95, 1986, 35 minutes; Rounder Records, One Camp Street, Cambridge, MA 02140, 800-443-4727)

DESCRIPTION: A jumping, joyful jewel of a jamborce in which multitalented Marcy Marxer and friends revive old standards with vigor and verve.

COMMENTS: Ms. Marxer teams up with Cathy Fink for *Help Yourself* and *When the Rain Comes Down.*

Paw Paw Patch (2–6, LP, Cassette, $9.98, 1987, 30 minutes; American Melody Records, P.O. Box 270, Guilford, CT 06437, 203-457-0881)

DESCRIPTION: Singer/instrumentalist Phil Rosenthal, in his best bluegrass style, features a folkfest of favorites, such as "Mary Had a Little Lamb," "Looby Loo," and "Are You Sleeping."

COMMENTS: An earlier recording, *Turkey in the Straw*, offers a similar treasury of traditional tunes.

Peter, Paul, and Mommy (3–8, LP, Cassette, $9.98, 1969, 36 minutes; Chinaberry Book Service, 2780 Via Orange Way, Spring Valley, CA 91978, 800-776-2242)

DESCRIPTION: Peter, Paul, and Mary, the folk stars who immortalized "Blowin' in the Wind," "If I Had a Hammer," and many more, perform music of their own ("Puff the Magic Dragon") and others (Tom Paxton's "The Marvelous Toy," Shel Silverstein's "Boa Constrictor") on this all-time best seller.

COMMENTS: *Sesame Street in Harmony* presents other top entertainers singing their favorite children's songs.

Stories and Songs for Little Children (3–7, Cassette, $9.98, 1990, 40 minutes; Windy Audio, P.O. Box 553, Fairview, NC 28730, 800-63STORY)

DESCRIPTION: The folk hero, Pete Seeger, who has been writing and performing for 50 years, transmits a bit of Americana with such songs as "Skip to My Loo" and "She'll Be Coming Round the Mountain." Also included is the much-loved "Abiyoyo," a tale based on an African legend that tells how a father and son save a town from a wicked giant.

COMMENTS: More by this inimitable, banjo-picking artist: *American Folk Songs for Children* and *Birds, Beasts, Bugs and Little Fishes*.

Play Songs/Quiet Songs

Hello Everybody! (1–4, Cassette, $7.95, 1986, 40 minutes; A Gentle Wind, P.O. Box 3103, Albany, NY 12203-0103, 518-436-0391)

DESCRIPTION: Rachel Buchman performs playsongs, lullabies, rhymes, and fingerplays in a friendly, comforting, award-winning recording that focuses on the everyday events and world of the toddler.

COMMENTS: Good resource for home or day-care setting.

Little Friends for Little Folks (2–5, Cassette, $7.95, 1986, 35 minutes; A Gentle Wind, P.O. Box 3103, Albany, NY 12203-0103, 518-436-0391)

DESCRIPTION: Janice Buckner will have kids clucking like chickens, croaking like frogs, and tooting like trains with her jaunty music, repetitive stories and rhymes, echo songs, and silly sound effects.

COMMENTS: This recording lends itself to creative and dramatic expression.

Lullaby Magic (2–5, Cassette, $9.95, 1985, 42 minutes; Discovery Music, 5554 Calhoun Ave., Van Nuys, CA 91401, 800-451-5175)

DESCRIPTION: Joanie Bartels weaves her own kind of magic in these sleepytime songs that range from Brahms to the Beatles. Like the others in this collection, the tape has a vocal version on one side and instrumentals only on the reverse. A lyrics sheet is included.

COMMENTS: Used by many hospitals and day-care centers, this series deals with such everyday activities as dancing, *Dancin'*

Magic, playing, *Sillytime Magic,* riding, *Travelin' Magic,* and washing, *Bathtime Magic.*

Makin' Music (2–6, LP, Cassette, $9.95, 1989, 45 minutes; Musical Munchkins, P.O. Box 356, Pound Ridge, NY 10576, 914-764-8568)

DESCRIPTION: The marvelous Musical Munchkins, made up of Chris Patella, Eileen Oddo, and George Rabbi, present a medley of rounds, rhythms, and games for singing and swinging.

COMMENTS: A lyrics sheet is included; a 60-page correlated teacher's guide and idea book is also available.

Shake It to the One That You Love the Best: Play Songs and Lullabies from Black Musical Traditions (3–7, Cassette/Songbook, $15.95; Cassette only, $10.95, 1990, 43 minutes; JTG, 1024C 18th Ave. South, Nashville, TN 37212, 800-222-2584)

DESCRIPTION: Warm, wonderful numbers derived from African, Creole, and Caribbean cultures are delivered by leading artists in a variety of styles—jazz, reggae, gospel, classical, and rhythm and blues.

COMMENTS: The songbook presents piano arrangements, guitar chords, and illustrations of African-American family life.

Star Dreamer: Nightsongs and Lullabies (Birth–3, LP, Cassette, $9; CD, $12, 1988, 40 minutes; Alcazar, P.O. Box 429, Waterbury, VT 05676, 800-541-9904)

DESCRIPTION: The crystal-clear voice of Priscilla Herdman, the tranquil music, and such sweet sounds of "Brahm's Lullaby" and "Goodnight Irene" will have any toddler nodding off in no time.

COMMENTS: Some other sleep-inducing selections not mentioned elsewhere: *Earth Mother Lullabies, Lullabies from Around the World, Lullabies Go Jazz,* and *Lullaby Berceuse.*

Fun and Learning

Holidays and Special Times (2–6, LP, Cassette, $10.98; CD, $13.98, 1989, 30 minutes; Youngheart Records, P.O. Box 6017, Cypress, CA 90630, 800-444-4287)

DESCRIPTION: Celebrations take center stage as Greg (Scelsa) and Steve (Millang) commemorate Thanksgiving, Christmas, Easter, Martin Luther King Day, Valentine's Day, Halloween, and birthdays with a contemporary, pop-rock sound that extends enjoyment and appreciation of special occasions.

COMMENTS: Their widely selling four-volume *We All Live Together* helps develop motor skills, basic concepts, and social interaction; their *Kids in Motion* video encourages exercise and movement.

I Know the Colors in the Rainbow (3–5, LP, Cassette, $10.95, 1981, 36 minutes; Educational Activities, P.O. Box 87, Baldwin, NY 11510, 800-645-3739)

DESCRIPTION: For over 35 years, Ella Jenkins has been introducing children to music, rhythms, instruments, and stories of other cultures. In this time-honored recording, she is joined by the St. Vincent De Paul Center Children's Chorus in listening and participation songs that focus on colors, tones, sounds, customs, and languages.

COMMENTS: Some of this renowned singer's best-loved recordings are *And One and Two, Travelin' with Ella Jenkins,* and *You'll Sing a Song and I'll Sing a Song.*

My First Concert (4–8, LP, Cassette, $14.95, 1986, 35 minutes; Rochester Philharmonic Orchestra, 108 East Ave., Rochester, NY 14604, 716-454-2620)

DESCRIPTION: A "meet-the-orchestra" recording by Isaiah Jackson and the Rochester Philharmonic in which youngsters learn about instruments and their sounds, and hear sure-to-please pieces from classical to classic tunes and nursery rhymes. A booklet with pictures of the instruments is included.

COMMENTS: Good classical recordings for children under 4 are scarce. Instead personal favorites or standards, such as *Peter and the Wolf* or *Flight of the Bumblebee,* should be shared.

Sing A to Z (3–6, Cassette, $8.98; CD, $12.98, 1991, 65 minutes; A&M, 800-925-7272; for further information, write to 1416 N. LaBrea Ave., Hollywood, CA 90028)

DESCRIPTION: Sharon, Lois, and Bram, the award-winning trio of audio, video, and Nickelodeon's *Elephant Show,* meander musically through the alphabet (and sprinkle in some poems and jokes for added merriment). *Mainly Mother Goose,* nursery rhymes with songs and finger games, is another too-good-to-miss recording.

COMMENTS: Any of the following are also excellent choices: *Elephant Show, Singing and Swinging, Smorgasbord,* and *Stay Tuned. Sleep Over* and *Who Stole the Cookies* get the video vote.

Popular Favorites

All for Freedom (3 and up, Cassette, $9.98; CD, $12.98, 1989, 47 minutes; Music for Little People, P.O. Box 1460, Redway, CA 95560, 800-346-4445)

DESCRIPTION: Sweet Honey in the Rock, a powerful women's quintet, tenders a triumphant tribute to African-American music and roots in a rich repertoire of folk, blues, jazz, freedom, gospel, and African songs and stories.

COMMENTS: Lyrics are included in this first children's album from the socially conscious, internationally acclaimed group.

Animal Crackers (2–5, Cassette, $8.98, 1990, 38 minutes; Alcazar, P.O. Box 429, Waterbury, VT 05676, 800-541-9904)

DESCRIPTION: Tasty tunes and adorable airs about animals abound in this award-winning album by the satiny-singing, dulcimer-playing Kevin Roth.

COMMENTS: Roth's *Lullabies for Little Dreamers* and *The Sandman* arc both super-soporific; *Unbearable Bears* is for teddy lovers.

Baby Beluga (2–5, LP, Cassette, CD, $9.95, 1990, 32 minutes; Troubadour Records, 1075 Cambie Street, Vancouver, B.C., Canada V6B5L7, 604-682-8698; distributed in USA by MCA Records)

DESCRIPTION: The phenomenon of children's music, Raffi is a gifted singer and songwriter whose sensitive, sophisticated lyrics stress people, nature, and the environment. *Baby Beluga,* a tender tale of a baby whale, and *Singable Songs for the Very Young,* a million-copy seller, are not to be missed.

COMMENTS: Other exceptional audios are *The Christmas Album; Everything Grows; One Light, One Sun; Rise and Shine;* and *A Young Children's Concert.*

A Car Full of Songs (3–6, Cassette, $9.98, 1992, 45 minutes; Mailbox Music, P.O. Box 341, Rye, NY 10580, 800-331-5269)

DESCRIPTION: The key to trouble-free travel might just be timeless Tom Paxton with "Are We There Yet?" and almost 20 others certain to keep things moving and relieve the tedium of long trips.

COMMENTS: *The Marvelous Toy* and *Peanut Butter Pie* are two more from this enduring folk artist.

Collections (3–6, Cassette, $8.98, 1990, 54 minutes; Alcazar, P.O. Box 429, Waterbury, VT 05676, 800-541-9904)

DESCRIPTION: Fred Penner, who turns simple everyday experiences into joyous happenings, highlights some of his hits (including his signature song "The Cat Came Back") on this terrific tape.

COMMENTS: Also recommended are the tune-filled *Polka Dot Pony, Special Delivery,* and *A House for Me*, a musical interpretation of Mary Ann Hoberman's book.

Deep in the Jungle (3–7, LP, Cassette, $9.95, 1987, 38 minutes; Shadow Play, P.O. Box 180476, Austin, TX 78718, 800-274-8804)

DESCRIPTION: Family-oriented songs, memorable sound effects, and easy-to-learn choruses make exploring with Joe Scruggs an adventure. His genial manner and music *(Abracadabra, Bahamas Pajamas, Jungle)* capture hearts and honors.

COMMENTS: *Traffic Jams* is especially good for restless kids during long car rides; *Joe's First Video* is a "playmation" masterpiece.

Grandma Slid Down the Mountain (3–6, LP, Cassette, $9; CD, $15, 1987, 40 minutes; Rounder Records, 1 Camp Street, Cambridge, MA 02140, 800-443-4727)

DESCRIPTION: A roundup of folk, country, and contemporary music by the versatile Cathy Fink has kids yodeling and joining in, with such fun-filled songs as "A Flea in a Fly in a Flu."

COMMENTS: An accompanying booklet provides song lyrics, activities, and historical background material.

Mail Myself to You (3–5, LP, Cassette, $9; CD, $15, 1988, 40 minutes; Rounder Records, One Camp Street, Cambridge, MA 02140, 800-433-4727)

DESCRIPTION: John McCutcheon gets a stamp of approval for this lively "special delivery" filled with upbeat arrangements of songs old and new. Comes with a coloring book and lyrics.

COMMENTS: *Howjadoo,* an earlier release, also contains spirited traditional and original songs.

Mother Earth (2–5, Cassette, $8.98; CD, $12.98, 1991, 36 minutes; A&M, 800-925-7272; for further information, write to 1416 N. La Brea Ave., Hollywood, CA 90028)

DESCRIPTION: On this clever, comical, conservation-oriented cassette, Tom Chapin shows his concern for life, nature, and the environment.

COMMENTS: Other notable, caring collections: *Family Tree* and *Moonboat.*

Pass the Coconut (2–5, Cassette, $8.98, 1991, 43 minutes; A&M, 800-925-7272; for further information, write to 1416 N. LaBrea Ave., Hollywood, CA 90028)

DESCRIPTION: A colorful compilation of child-related songs ("Spend a Little Time with Grandpa," "Glad I Got My Boots On") are charmingly delivered by Frank Cappelli, the host of television's *Cappelli and Company.*

COMMENTS: The video *All Aboard the Train* is engineered around childhood experiences, as are the audios *On Vacation* and *You Wanna Be a Duck.*

Peek-a-Boo (2–5, LP, Cassette, $10.95, 1990, 30 minutes; Educational Activities, P.O. Box 87, Baldwin, NY 11510, 800-645-3739)

DESCRIPTION: The prolific composer and singer Hap Palmer, with more than 200 songs and 30 recordings to his credit, presents imaginative, toe-tapping tunes about experiences, challenges, and feelings of the younger set. A 25-page songbook is included.

COMMENTS: Much of this artist's music, reflecting his early childhood background, focuses on improving creativity, movement, and early learning skills. His *Babysong* is a must for toddlers under 3.

Tickles You (3–6, LP, Cassette, $9.98, 1980, 49 minutes; Lightyear Entertainment, 350 Fifth Ave., Suite 5101, New York, NY 10118, 800-229-7867)

DESCRIPTION: This first release from Gary Rosen and Bill Schontz, the dynamic duo known as Rosenschontz, continues to tickle both parents and preschoolers alike (and it is still their biggest seller). Superb songs with witty, inventive lyrics and creative instrumentation set a standard that's hard to equal.

COMMENTS: Peerless picks by the same pair: *Rock'N'Roll Teddy Bear, Share It,* and the video *The Teddy Bear's Picnic.*

FREE OR INEXPENSIVE MATERIALS

The American Music Conference, 303 East Wacker Drive, Suite 1214, Chicago, IL 60601.

The following brochures are available free of charge with a business-size (#10), self-addressed, stamped envelope; two brochures require additional postage.

Music and Your Child: The Importance of Music to Children's Development. The positive effects of music on children's social, intellectual, and physical development.

Message to Parents. Benefits of music, selecting a teacher, and supporting and encouraging music study.

National Association for the Education of Young Children, 1834 Connecticut Avenue, N.W., Washington, DC 20009-5786, 800-424-2460.

Music in Our Lives: The Early Years. Dorothy T. McDonald. Significance and development of musical skills, and how to plan meaningful and enjoyable musical experiences. $4.

Preschool Publications, P.O. Box 1851, Garden City, NY 11530-0816, 516-742-9557.

Music . . . Sounds Like Fun. A very informative back issue (April, 1987) from *Parent and Preschooler Newsletter*. Suggestions for nurturing music appreciation, tips for parents, some formal approaches to teaching music, and an excellent chart of music development. $1.25.

AUDIO CATALOGS

Some companies produce excellent catalogs that provide an idea of the breadth and depth of recordings available for young children. These catalogs contain descriptive information about titles and performers that can help in determining whether selections are appropriate. Many firms maintain a toll-free telephone number and are pleased to answer questions and provide suggestions. The companies listed below are reputable, helpful, and have good return and exchange policies.

A Gentle Wind, P.O. Box 3103, Albany, NY 12203-0103, 518-436-0391.

Alcazar's Kiddie Kat, P.O. Box 429, South Main Street, Waterbury, VT 05676, 802-244-8657, 800-541-9904.

Children's Book and Music Center, 2500 Santa Monica Boulevard, Santa Monica, CA 90404, 213-829-0215, 800-443-1856, Fax: 213-829-0836.

Chinaberry Book Service, 2830 Via Orange Way, Suite B, Spring Valley, CA 91978, 619-670-5200, 800-776-2242, Fax: 619-670-5203.

Educational Activities, Inc., P.O. Box 87, Baldwin, NY 11510, 516-223-4666, 800-645-3739, Fax: 516-623-9282.

Educational Record Center, Building 400, Suite 400, 1575 Northside Drive, N.W., Atlanta, GA 30318-4298, 404-352-8282, 800-438-1637, Fax: 404-351-2544.

Kimbo Educational, P.O. Box 477P, Long Branch, NJ 07740-0477, 908-229-4949, 800-631-2187, Fax: 908-870-3340.

Listening Library, One Park Avenue, Old Greenwich, CT 06870-1727, 800-243-4504, Fax: 203-698-1998.

Music for Little People, P.O. Box 1460, Redway, CA 95560, 800-346-4445.

Upbeat, 163 Joralemon Street, Suite 1250, Brooklyn, NY 11201, 718-522-5349, 800-872-3288.

Chapter 2

Books

Reading is the foundation of knowledge and success, the key to pleasure and beauty. Books provide endless opportunities for enrichment, entertainment, satisfaction, and fulfillment.

Learning to read begins at a very early age, years before a child ever enters a classroom. Starting in the home, children acquire the language, knowledge, and attitudes that form the basis for reading. Parents are a child's first and most important teachers. They exert a powerful influence on the child's reading development.

ON THE ROAD TO READING: HOW PARENTS/CAREGIVERS CAN HELP

One of the most precious gifts a parent can give a child is a love of books. The following suggestions will help to nurture this love and to turn youngsters on to the joys of reading:

1. *Read aloud.* A National Commission on Reading reported that the single most important activity for eventual success in reading is reading aloud to children.[1] This should be started as early as possible—during infancy is not too soon. Kids who are read to at a very young age are much more likely to become "hooked on books" than those who are not. Bedtime is often the

favorite "read-aloud" time, but any time is great for the warmth and intimacy of this valuable shared experience.

2. *Set an example.* Children are great imitators. The more parents read, the more they share their enthusiasm for a good book, and the more likely the child will view reading as a desirable, valuable activity. The home should be filled with all kinds of reading material, including books, magazines, newspapers, etc., so that right from the start reading will be a natural part of the child's life.

3. *Take time to talk.* The ability to use language is critical for reading achievement. Talking expands vocabulary, increases concepts, and aids thinking and learning. Parents should be alert to naturally occurring opportunities, such as when doing chores or going on errands, in which they can chat with their youngsters. Language should not be oversimplified; even the youngest child is able to catch on to the meaning of big, unfamiliar words. It is also important to listen patiently; letting children complete their thoughts without being cut off aids self-expression and self-esteem.

4. *Expand knowledge.* The more information a youngster has, the greater his or her chances of becoming a successful reader. Varied experiences provide good background understanding and mental links to the printed word. Even such everyday activities as shopping and taking neighborhood walks, and visiting parks, zoos, and museums increase knowledge and spark interest and curiosity.

5. *Write on!* Writing helps a child make the connection between print and speech, learn about letters and words, and see a real reason for reading. Preschoolers can create scrapbooks,

greeting cards, letters, thank-you notes, and dictate stories and journals. Good writing materials include pencils, crayons, colored pens, wide- and thin-tipped markers, lined and unlined paper, and even a typewriter or computer if available. Beginning attempts may include such invented spelling as "i c u." These early efforts should be praised; it is unwise to insist on conventional spelling or expect neat, well-formed letters at this stage. In time, the child's writing and spelling will improve, as will his or her reading ability.

6. *Link up with the library.* Librarians are wonderful allies in raising readers, and many libraries offer special programs and story hours for the preschooler. Youngsters should be encouraged to select their own books, without rushing, to enjoy the pleasure and adventure of browsing.

7. *Launch a library.* Few things stimulate a love of reading more than the ownership of a few beloved books. These should be stored in a special place, such as a bookcase, a shelf, or something as simple as a large box with the child's name on it. A quiet, comfortable, well-lighted place where a child can curl up with a good book is also conducive to instilling the reading habit.

8. *Tune out TV.* Many parents and educators, concerned about the staggering amount of time preschoolers spend watching television, recommend that TV be monitored and limited to one or two hours daily. Whenever possible, parents should share the viewing with their youngsters, discuss and ask questions about the program, and relate it to other situations and experiences.

9. *Reinforce reading.* Activities such as storytelling, dramatization, role playing, puppetry, and game playing actually help to

improve readiness (see chapters on children's toys and resource books). It is not always necessary for parents or caregivers to participate. Preschoolers are often happy just to have someone available to answer questions, perhaps offer an occasional suggestion, and admire what they do.

10. *Seize the moment.* Capitalize on the child's interests, concerns, or a special event to motivate reading (see section "Topical Titles" for appropriate books).

The above suggestions will help make reading as joyous and successful as possible. It is important to remember that the goal is to develop positive attitudes rather than to focus on improving skills. Pressuring or pushing the preschooler, even with the best of intentions, can have negative results. Instead, praising the child for efforts and instilling pride in accomplishments will improve self-confidence and further the desire to grow and learn!

WHAT TO LOOK FOR

With so much to choose from, parents and caregivers are often unsure which books are best for their preschooler. The following tables provide guidance in finding a good match at each stage of development. The tables contain information about characteristics of children from ages 2 through 5, implications for book selection, helpful hints, and specific titles for every level.

The distinctions, however, are intended as general guidelines and often overlap age groupings. Moreover, each child is unique, develops at his or her own pace, and has his or her own needs, interests, and abilities. In the final analysis, the child is the ultimate judge. If he or she likes a book, then it is the "right" one.

Age 2

Characteristics	Types of Books	Suggestions	Examples
Seeks security; builds trust.	Stories of love and caring.	Read aloud with child snuggled close.	*More More More*—Williams
Expands language; builds vocabulary; develops concepts.	Simple information books about words, colors, shapes, counting.	Talk, name, describe. Provide variety; don't overdo "educational" books.	*Mouse Paint*—Walsh *Fish Eyes*—Ehlert
Focuses on self and familiar experiences.	Stories of activities, routines, home life with which toddler can identify.	Make up stories about the toddler's day. Have child fill in gaps, make up own story.	*This Is Betsy*—Wolde *Jesse Bear*—Carlstrom
Enjoys involvement and exploration.	Books with opportunities for lifting flaps, moving, and feeling objects.	Encourage pointing to pictures, turning pages. Durable board books are good now.	*Where's Spot*—Hill *Wheels on the Bus*—Zelinsky
Loves repetition, rhythm, and rhyme.	Books with recurring words and actions. Mother Goose, nursery rhymes.	Be prepared to read (and reread) favorites. Have child join in, repeat, complete rhymes.	*Brown Bear, Brown Bear*—Martin *Little Dog Laughed*—Cousins
Moves frequently; limited attention span.	Short, fast-paced action stories. Picture books with little or no text.	Limit each session to 10–15 minutes. Have child tell story from the pictures.	*Have You Seen My Duckling*—Tafuri *Where Does Brown Bear Go*—Weiss

Age 3

Characteristics	Types of Books	Suggestions	Examples
Extends language skills and concept development.	Longer stories with more involved plots. Counting, alphabet, "concept" books.	Continue reading aloud; share, discuss, question.	*Chicka Chicka Boom Boom*—Martin & Archambault *Bugs in a Box*—Carter
Takes pleasure in accomplishments.	Stories demonstrating growth, initiative.	Praise attempts and achievements.	*Carrot Seed*—Krauss
Enjoys rhymes.	Simple poems, songs, rhymes.	Encourage chiming in and memorization.	*Read-Aloud Rhymes*—Prelutsky
Appreciates humor.	Funny books with silly language, nonsense words, ridiculous situations.	Giggle, chuckle, and laugh together. Enjoyment is key!	*Sheep in a Shop*—Shaw *Cat in the Hat*—Seuss
Engages in make-believe.	Books involving imaginative play and personification of toys and animals.	Provide opportunities and props for dramatic play.	*Corduroy*—Freeman *Caps for Sale*—Slobodkina
Develops fears of the dark, animals, strangers, unknown situations.	Books about typical worries and concerns, e.g., nursery school, monsters.	Offer comfort and reassurance. Books help explore, explain, and ease fears.	*My Nursery School*—Rockwell *Can't Sleep Little Bear?*—Waddell

Age 4

Characteristics	Types of Books	Suggestions	Examples
Uses more sophisticated language to describe, find out, share.	Books with diverse language styles, and more detail and description.	Have children respond, predict, compare, contrast, retell, make up stories.	*Abuela*—Dorros *Mama, Do You Love Me*—Joosse
Matures; handles more complex material; increases attention span.	Increased variety and length of books. More advanced "concept" books.	Continue reading aloud; books involving size, shape, distance, classification.	*All about Where*—Hoban *First Look at Time*—Shott & Oliver
Becomes more assertive and self-reliant.	Stories with themes of dependence/independence; adult-child conflicts; determination.	Permit more freedom in decision-making (selecting books, clothing); encourage and praise efforts.	*Runaway Bunny*—Brown *Tale of Peter Rabbit*—Potter *Little Engine That Could*—Piper
Seeks information about the world; inquisitive.	Books about other people and places; how things work.	Take walks; visit interesting places. Use books to preview and follow-up.	*Machines at Work*—Barton *Tools*—Shone
Expands imagination; enjoys fantasy; exaggerates.	Stories with absurd situations; simple folktales.	Provide examples of reality and fantasy to help children see difference.	*Where the Wild Things Are*—Sendak *Goldilocks*—Marshall
Becomes more social.	Books about friendship and play.	Provide opportunities for socialization.	*Will I Have a Friend*—Cohen

Age 5

Characteristics	Types of Books	Suggestions	Examples
Expands use of books. "Reads" independently; learns mechanics of reading (front to back, left to right, top to bottom); recognizes words by sight; identifies letters and sounds.	Rich and varied mix of books. Longer texts with strong plots. Well-developed characters; increasing dialogue and detail. Illustrations differing in style and medium.	Encourage dramatization, writing, bookmaking, illustration, reading games. Draw attention to reading direction by sweeping hand along line. Praise word recognition; resist temptation to "drill."	*Make Way for Ducklings*—McCloskey *10 Little Rabbits*—Grossman & Long *Rosie's Walk*—Hutchins *Borreguita and the Coyote*—Aardema *I Spy*—Marzollo *Napping House*—Wood
Begins kindergarten.	Books that prepare child for school.	Discuss what to expect; reassure.	*Starting School*—Ahlberg
Extends horizons; increases interest in "real" world.	Books about the neighborhood, community, city.	Continue outings for firsthand experiences. Use books as resource.	*Truck Song*—Siebert *Freight Train*—Crews
Grows emotionally; wants to please; cooperative.	Stories of consideration, helping others, accepting responsibility.	Be appreciative; reward good behavior. Assign chores (clearing table, etc.).	*Chair for My Mother*—Williams *When I Am Old with You*—Johnson
Increases awareness of personal problems.	Books dealing with such sensitive subjects as death and divorce.	Do not hide sad events; explain as simply as possible. Books can help address emotional issues.	*When a Pet Dies*—Rogers *Daddy*—Caines

BOOKS ABOUND

One of the fastest-growing segments in publishing today, books for the very young, is flourishing. They come in all sizes, shapes, textures, and design. There are tiny, oversized, pop-up and pull-out, and "scratch and sniff" books. There are books made of cloth, plastic, and cardboard, and books that talk, make noises, and play tunes. There are also book–cassette combinations, personalized computer-generated books, and toy books of every conceivable kind. There are even those that come with real seeds and cameras, float in the bathtub, and glow in the dark!

Preschool literature also takes many forms. Picture books combine both text and illustration to tell a story. Some books have no words, letting youngsters "read" the story from the pictures. Other books, known as predictable books, contain repetitive words or patterns that encourage children to join in and anticipate what will happen next. Very young children also enjoy participation books—those that provide opportunities for hands-on involvement, i.e., touching, manipulating, moving, and smelling. Whatever the type, books should invite, delight, and excite!

TOPICAL TITLES: THE RIGHT BOOK AT THE RIGHT TIME

For ease and convenience in finding the perfect book for a particular occasion, the best preschool titles have been grouped in 13 main topics that are of special interest and concern to preschoolers. The books are all recipients of many distinguished awards, but in the interest of space, only the prestigious Newbery Medal for writing and the Caldecott Medal for illustration, are indicated. Other suggested titles by the same author are included in the "Comments" section. Books marked with an asterisk are those all-time favorite, not-to-be-missed books that were recommended most frequently by the sources listed in the "References" section. Prices are included as a general guide but may vary according to location and store; the notation (P) signifies a paperback edition.

Alphabet Books

Alphabet books, traditional fare for tots, teach letter identification, sequence, and sounds in a never-ending, ever-new variety of ways. These range from the simple matching of a letter with an object to more complex story, rhyme, and game formats. Here is a sampling of the best.

A Is for Animals (David Pelham, Simon & Schuster, 1991, 13 pp., $14.95)

DESCRIPTION: This "26 pop-up surprises" animal ABC is ingeniously designed and enormously appealing. Every page has two flaps, each printed with its own upper- and lower-case letter. When opened, brightly colored, familiar and not-so-familiar animals and birds of all sorts spring out to greet the reader.

COMMENTS: Good for learning about animals as well as the alphabet. This book will require special care and handling to keep it in shape.

Alphabatics (Suse MacDonald, Bradbury/Macmillan, 1986, 56 pp., $15.95)

DESCRIPTION: Ingenious twists and turns of letters into pictures—A is turned topsy-turvy into an animal-filled ark, P zooms off to become a plane—open up new ways of looking at the alphabet.

COMMENTS: As kids hunt for the original shapes in the final formations, they get lots of visual reinforcement learning the letters.

Alphabears: An ABC Book (Kathleen Hague, illustrated by Michael Hague, Holt, 1985, 32 pp., $12.95; (P) Holt, 1991, $4.95)

DESCRIPTION: Twenty-six huggable bears (from Amanda to Zak) and quaint, old-fashioned charm permeate rhyming alphabet couplets.

COMMENTS: *Numbears* is the companion counting book.

Animal Alphabet (Bert Kitchen, Dial, 1984, 32 pp., $13.95; (P) Dial, 1988, $4.95)

DESCRIPTION: Commanding black letters, intertwined with striking, exotic animals, jump out of white pages to imprint themselves upon young minds. Answers to the animals' identities are at the end.

COMMENTS: *Animal Numbers* is the equally visually compelling numerical counterpart.

Anno's Alphabet: An Adventure in Imagination (Mitsumasa Anno, Crowell, 1975, 64 pp., $13.95; (P) Trophy, 1988, $5.95)

DESCRIPTION: Each left-hand page shows a capital letter that looks as though it's made of wood. Every right-hand page has a color illustration of an object beginning with that letter. While some objects may be known, others will be new in these alphabetical illusions.

COMMENTS: Additional figures in the decorative frames are perfect for playing ever-popular "search-and-find" games.

Chicka Chicka Boom Boom (Bill Martin, Jr., and John Archambault, illustrated by Lois Ehlert, Simon & Schuster, 1989, 36 pp., $13.95)

DESCRIPTION: Bright, bold letters scamper up the coconut tree, but when the tree can't hold them, Chicka Chicka Boom Boom, they tumble on down again. Some are slightly bruised, *M* is looped, *N* is stooped, and *O* is twisted alley-oop in this rhythmic alphabet chant.

COMMENTS: Also available on audio for alphabet amplification.

On Market Street (Arnold Lobel, illustrated by Anita Lobel, Greenwillow, 1981, 40 pp., $13.95; (P) Mulberry, 1989, $4.95)

DESCRIPTION: A shopping spree along Market Street sets the stage for learning the alphabet. Each letter is represented by an object to be bought, and illustrated by a vendor elaborately fashioned from that object. *D,* for example, is represented by a doughnut and a lady designed from doughnuts.

COMMENTS: This book, inspired by seventeenth-century French trade engravings, can prompt children to make their own alphabet people.

Animals

Preschoolers seem to have a natural affinity for animals and often identify with their feelings and antics. The following stories represent some of our most beloved fictional animal characters.

Curious George (H. A. Rey, Houghton Mifflin, 1973, 56 pp., $12.95; (P) Houghton Mifflin, 1973, $3.95)

DESCRIPTION: George is a cute little monkey who does the kinds of things little kids are likely to do as they explore their world. His curiosity causes complications that have delighted readers for more than half a century, while also teaching that actions have consequences.

COMMENTS: Monkeyshines continue in countless *Curious* capers.

Harry the Dirty Dog (Gene Zion, illustrated by Margaret Bloy Graham, HarperCollins, 1956, 32 pp., $13.95; (P) Trophy, 1976, $3.95)

DESCRIPTION: Like many kids, Harry hates baths. But he learns that being dirty can sometimes have its disadvantages.

COMMENTS: Harry's dogged deeds are also detailed in *No Roses for Harry, The Plant Sitter,* and more.

Make Way for Ducklings (Robert McCloskey, Viking Penguin, 1941, 64 pp., $12.95; (P) Puffin, 1976, $3.95)

DESCRIPTION: The Mallards are just a normal family concerned about a safe place to raise their kids. When they find one, they also find a friendly policeman who feeds them and looks out for them with some help from his friends on the force. Since policemen are so nice to ducks, they're sure to be even nicer to children.

COMMENTS: Both this and 50-year-old veteran *Blueberries for Sal,* a maternal mix-up that's a "must," are Caldecott Medal winners.

★Millions of Cats (Wanda Gag, Coward, 1928, 32 pp., $9.95; (P) Coward, 1977, $3.95)

DESCRIPTION: Children quickly learn to repeat the refrain "Hundreds of cats, thousands of cats, millions and billions and trillions of cats." Each one as pretty as the next, but in the end, it's a humble, scraggly kitten who makes the old man and old woman happy.

COMMENTS: This Newbery Honor Books winner was the first picture book for children published in the United States. The rhythmic, repetitive text is perfect for participation and dramatization.

★The Story of Babar (Jean de Brunhoff, Random House, 1937, 48 pp., $9.95; (P) Knopf, 1989, $4.95)

DESCRIPTION: The story of an orphaned baby elephant who lives royally among men, and then returns home to be crowned king, is a warm fantasy that children have always taken to their hearts.

COMMENTS: See video section for more mammoth merriment in *Babar the Elephant Comes to America.*

The Story of Ferdinand (Munro Leaf, illustrated by Robert Lawson, Viking, 1936, 76 pp., $11.95; (P) Puffin, 1988, $6.95)

DESCRIPTION: A sweet-tempered bull was stung by a bee, and it hurt so bad that he jumped and puffed and snorted and butted and pawed the ground. That was the start of Ferdinand's troubles, but all ends triumphantly in this peace-loving tale.

COMMENTS: This timeless treasure is a Caldecott Honor Book.

★*Where's Spot* (Eric Hill, Putnam, 1980, 22 pp., $10.95; (P) Crocodile, 1988, $10.95)

DESCRIPTION: That's the big question as children help search for a roly-poly puppy under every flap in this hands-on participation perennial.

COMMENTS: Tots adore Spot and all his sequels (*Spot's Birthday Party, Spot Goes to School,* etc.).

Bedtime

Bedtime stories provide comfort and reassurance that young children often need to help them face the dark and fall off to sleep. Bedtime reading, however, need not be restricted to "sleep" themes; many types of stories can be shared at this favorite reading-aloud time.

★*Bedtime for Frances* (Russell Hoban, illustrated by Garth Williams, HarperCollins, 1960, 32 pp., $12.95; (P) Trophy, 1976, $3.95)

DESCRIPTION: It's not that this engaging badger doesn't want to go to bed, she's just not very sleepy. Then she begins to wonder: Is that a giant in the corner? Will something with lots of legs come out of the crack in the ceiling?

COMMENTS: Every child has had at least one night like this, and parents and children will see themselves in Frances and her mom and dad.

Can't You Sleep, Little Bear? (Martin Waddell, illustrated by Barbara Firth, Candlewick, 1992, 32 pp., $14.95)

DESCRIPTION: A sleepless night in Bear Cave, in which a cub's bedtime fears are put to rest with patience and understanding.

COMMENTS: *There's a Nightmare in My Closet* is also about fear of the dark.

★*Goodnight Moon* (Margaret Wise Brown, illustrated by Clement Hurd, HarperCollins, 1947, 36 pp., $10.95; (P) Trophy, 1977, $3.95)

DESCRIPTION: In the waning light of day, a little bunny whispers goodnight to everything in his "great, green room." The magical illustrations of this all-time beloved bedtime book evoke a sense of peace and security.

COMMENTS: Toddlers enjoy chiming in, naming the objects, and spotting the little mouse in every picture.

★*Moonlight* (Jan Ormerod, Lothrop, 1982, 32 pp., $14.95; (P) Puffin, 1984, $3.50)

DESCRIPTION: A little girl has her dinner, a bath, a story, is tucked in, but then finds one excuse after another to delay going to sleep. The soft, delicate watercolors sensitively express the tenderness and warmth in this appealing tale.

COMMENTS: A companion book, *Sunshine,* portrays morning activities with the same family.

★*The Napping House* (Audrey Wood, illustrated by Don Wood, Harcourt Brace Jovanovich, 1984, 32 pp., $13.95)

DESCRIPTION: A snoring granny sleeps in her cozy bed as a storm rages outside. One by one, in this cumulative rhyme, she is joined by a dreamy child, dozing dog, and other drowsy animals until an explosive awakening.

COMMENTS: Other gloriously illustrated books include *Piggies* and *King Bidgood's in the Bathtub.*

*Ten, Nine, Eight (Molly Bang, Greenwillow, 1983, 24 pp., $13.95; (P) Mulberry, 1991, $3.95)

DESCRIPTION: A loving father prepares his daughter for bed by counting backwards from ten toes all washed and warm, to nine soft friends, to eight square windowpanes, to, finally, one girl all ready for bed.

COMMENTS: This Caldecott Honor Book also reinforces counting skills.

Tucking Mommy In (Morag Loh, illustrated by Donna Rawlins, Orchard/Watts, 1988, 40 pp., $13.95; (P) Orchard/Watts, 1991, $4.95)

DESCRIPTION: Here is a bedtime story with a twist. Instead of mom putting the kids to bed, she's so exhausted that she falls asleep before they do. It takes some doing for the kids to get Mom tucked in, in her own bed, and then it's their turn when Dad gets home.

COMMENTS: Children (and parents, too) will chuckle at this humorous turnabout, and see that sometimes parents need help, too.

Where Does the Brown Bear Go? (Nicki Weiss, Greenwillow, 1989, 24 pp., $13.95; (P) Puffin, 1990, $3.95)

DESCRIPTION: When shadows fall, where do the cat, camel, and other creatures go? They all head for home, as animals (and little children) settle cozily off to sleep.

COMMENTS: A tranquil and serene, sure-to-please slumber inducer!

Child's World

Children love to read stories that mirror their own lives. Stories in this section focus on the family, feelings, first learnings, and familiar routines.

A, B, C, D, Tummy, Toes, Hands, Knees (B. G. Hennessy, illustrated by Wendy Watson, Viking Kestrel, 1989, 32 pp., $12.95; (P) Puffin, 1991, $3.95)

DESCRIPTION: Right on the title page, a little chap is seen getting out of bed, dragging his blanket behind him. From then on, this rollicking rhyme is filled with feeding, dressing, shopping, playing, hugging, and good-natured hi-jinks of a typical toddler's day.

COMMENTS: Having youngsters tell what they like best about their favorite activities strengthens oral expression.

Abuela (Arthur Dorros, illustrated by Elisa Kleven, Dutton, 1991, 40 pp., $13.95)

DESCRIPTION: The love between Rosalba and her grandmother, her *abuela,* soars in this high-flying, imaginative adventure set in New York City.

COMMENTS: The English narration is spiced with some Spanish phrases.

★*Alfie's Feet* (Shirley Hughes, Lothrop, 1983, 32 pp., $14.95; (P) Mulberry, 1988, $3.95)

DESCRIPTION: Walking and wearing shoes require learning some new things, as Alfie finds out when he gets some shiny new yellow boots. He splashes in puddles, stomps around the house, and discovers there's a difference between right and left.

COMMENTS: This book can be used to reinforce concepts of left and right. Other appealing Alfie stories: *Alfie Gets In First, Alfie Gives a Hand,* and *An Evening at Alfie's.*

Daddy (Jeannette Caines, illustrated by Ronald Himler, Harper-Collins, 1977, 32 pp., $12.95)

DESCRIPTION: Windy's daddy comes to get her every Saturday. They do special things together, like play games and go to the grocery store. Windy admits she gets wrinkles in her stomach worrying about Daddy at night or when she's in school, but when he comes on Saturday the wrinkles go away.

COMMENTS: This empathetic story may help children of divorced or separated parents deal with and discuss their feelings.

Jafta (Hugh Lewin, illustrated by Lisa Kipper, Carolrhoda, 1983, 24 pp., $8.95; (P) Lerner, 1989, $3.95)

DESCRIPTION: When Jafta, a little African boy, is happy, he purrs like a lion cub, skips like a spider, or laughs like a hyena. And when he is tired or cross (which isn't often), he stamps like an elephant. Although Jafta describes his emotions by comparing them to wild animals, children can see that they have the same feelings no matter where they live.

COMMENTS: Others in the satisfying series: *Jafta and the Wedding, Jafta's Father, Jafta's Mother,* and *Jafta: The Town.*

*Jesse Bear, What Will You Wear? (Nancy White Carlstrom, illustrated by Bruce Degen, Macmillan, 1986, 32 pp., $13.95)

DESCRIPTION: Jesse Bear is a cheerful little fellow who takes the question of what he'll wear with a touch of whimsy. From "shirt of red in the morning" to "dreams in his head" at night, this lilting romp describes a fanciful day of dress and exploration.

COMMENTS: This bear-child can be followed in *Better Not Get Wet, Jesse Bear* and *It's about Time, Jesse Bear.*

Mama, Do You Love Me? (Barbara M. Joosse, illustrated by Barbara Lavallee, Chronicle, 1991, 32 pp., $12.95)

DESCRIPTION: As a small Inuit girl tests the limits of her mother's love ("What if I put salmon in your parka, ran away and sang with the wolves?"), children realize that parental love is universal and unconditional.

COMMENTS: Text and images of Arctic life expand appreciation of another culture.

"More More More," Said the Baby (Vera B. Williams, Greenwillow, 1990, 32 pp., $12.95)

DESCRIPTION: A trio of multiethnic vignettes in which mama, daddy, and grandma play cuddling and tickling games with their much-loved babies. As Little Guy, Little Pumpkin, and Little Bird are swung, hugged, and kissed, they murmur, "More. More. More."

COMMENTS: This and *A Chair for My Mother* are superfine Caldecott Honor Books.

This Is Betsy (Gunilla Wolde, Random House, 1990, 24 pp., $4.95)

DESCRIPTION: Like all little kids, Betsy can be pretty silly. She knows the right way to get dressed, brush her hair, and drink her cocoa, but sometimes it's fun to do things a little differently. Children will see themselves in Betsy, who's really a very good little girl.

COMMENTS: Other titles in this series of small, bright books that focus on preschooler experiences are *Betsy's Baby Brother, Betsy's First Day at Nursery School, Betsy and the Doctor.*

When I Am Old with You (Angela Johnson, illustrated by David Soman, Orchard/Watts, 1990, 32 pp., $14.95)

DESCRIPTION: In this poignant story, a small boy, who has not yet grasped concepts of time and aging, expresses his deeply felt wish to be always beside his grandaddy.

COMMENTS: *Tell Me a Story* and *One of Three* are also heart-warmers.

Concepts

Concept books, designed primarily to extend children's knowledge, focus on such topics as color, size, shape, time, and space relationships. Strictly speaking, alphabet and counting books are also concept books, but because of their number and popularity with preschoolers they are being presented separately. Children learn best from direct, firsthand experiences; books should supplement, not substitute for, these experiences.

All about Where (Tana Hoban, Greenwillow, 1991, 32 pp., $13.95)

DESCRIPTION: The camera is turned on to "locational" words (e.g., above, across, against) with museum-quality photographs that ogle the eye and the mind. *Is It Red? Is It Yellow? Is It Blue?, Of Colors and Things,* and *26 Letters and 99 Cents* are just three more of this author's 25+ superlative concept books.

COMMENTS: "Simon-says"-type games in which children are

told to put hands above their heads, behind their neck, and below their knees offer additional language practice.

I Spy: A Book of Picture Riddles (Photographs by Walter Wick, riddles by Jean Marzollo, Scholastic, 1992, 34 pp., $10.95)

DESCRIPTION: As kids explore the exceptional pictures, find the hidden objects, solve the riddles, and play "I Spy," they'll improve language, perception, counting, and thinking skills.

COMMENTS: Creating original rhymes and riddles continue the fun and learning.

Mouse Paint (Ellen Stoll Walsh, Harcourt Brace Jovanovich, 1989, 32 pp., $11.95; (P) Harcourt, 1991, $18.95 (Big Book)

DESCRIPTION: Three jolly mice dip in and out of primary paint jars. As they dance in each other's puddles, they see the colors mix to make orange, green, and purple. Or as they put it, "yellow feet in a blue puddle make green!"

COMMENTS: Preschoolers should prove these precepts with their own jars of red, yellow, and blue paint.

My First Look at Time (Photographs by Stephen Shott and Stephen Oliver, Random House, 1991, 20 pp., $6.95)

DESCRIPTION: Concepts of time and the clock are introduced by vivid photos that chronicle a typical day.

COMMENTS: *My First Look at* series explores many beginning concepts including *Seasons, Sizes, Shapes, Sorting,* and *Touch.*

Paddington's Opposites (Michael Bond, illustrated by John Lobban, Viking, 1991, 32 pp., $10.95)

DESCRIPTION: Paddington stands forlornly in the rain above

the caption *Wet,* but the next page shows him smiling under an umbrella for *Dry.* A plate loaded with marmalade sandwiches is labeled *Many; Few* is illustrated by only three remaining (and a bulging bear stomach).

COMMENTS: The lovable bear in his slouchy hat teaches other concepts in *Paddington's: ABC, 1,2,3,* and *Colors.*

Polar Bear, Polar Bear, What Do You Hear? (Bill Martin, Jr., illustrated by Eric Carle, Holt, 1991, 32 pp., $13.95)

DESCRIPTION: The emphasis is on animals and their distinctive sounds in a repetitive question-and-answer format that kids really take to. There are roaring lions, braying zebras, trumpeting elephants (plus young imitators) in this very noisy, magnificently illustrated zoo.

COMMENTS: This team concentrated on colors with their bestselling *★Brown Bear, Brown Bear, What Do You See?*

Shapes (John J. Reiss, Bradbury, 1982, 32 pp., $13.95; (P) Aladdin, 1987, $3.95)

DESCRIPTION: Squares change into cubes, triangles into pyramids, and circles into spheres in this dazzling ballet of kaleidoscopic shape transformations.

COMMENTS: Having a "shape search" (finding shapes around the house, in magazines) is a super sequel.

Counting

Counting books, which come in a wide variety of formats, concentrate on number identification, sequence, and basic mathematical concepts. Children learn best from real experiences, so opportunities for counting concrete objects, such as books, toys, crayons, napkins, etc., should be woven into the daily routine.

Fish Eyes (Lois Ehlert, Harcourt Brace Jovanovich, 1990, 36 pp., $14.95)

DESCRIPTION: Flipping, flashing, fantailed fish as well as striped, spotted, smiling species swim on by to nurture number sequencing. The electric color collages, the cut-out eyes, and the friendly guide make this a book that can be counted on again and again.

COMMENTS: Eye-catching, educational fare is also on the menu in *Eating the Alphabet, Growing Vegetable Soup,* and *Painting a Rainbow.*

Have You Seen My Duckling? (Nancy Tafuri, Greenwillow, 1984, 24 pp., $15.95; (P) Puffin, 1986, $3.95)

DESCRIPTION: Mama Duck searches all over the pond for her stray. As she questions each animal and fish in turn, eagle-eyed youngsters can catch glimpses of the missing duckling nearby.

COMMENTS: Both this Caldecott Honor Book and *Who's Counting?* contain considerable chances to practice number skills.

How Many Bugs in a Box? (David A. Carter, Simon & Schuster, 1988, 20 pp., $11.95)

DESCRIPTION: Lots of boxes (tall, small, square, thin, polka-dot) and silly bugs (that run, swim, eat, etc.) teach concepts of counting, color, size, and shape in an interactive pop-up and pull-out book that houses all sorts of surprises.

COMMENTS: The sequel, *More Bugs in Boxes,* centers on colors.

Moja Means One (Muriel Feelings, illustrated by Tom Feelings, Dial, 1987, 32 pp., $13.95; (P) Dial, 1976, $4.95)

DESCRIPTION: This Swahili counting book can be enjoyed on many levels. Younger children can count the trees, fish, instruments, etc., while older children will also appreciate seeing different aspects of East African life, and the number words printed phonetically in Swahili.

COMMENTS: *Jambo Means Hello* is the companion alphabet book.

1 Hunter (Pat Hutchins, Greenwillow, 1982, 24 pp., $13.95; (P) Mulberry, $3.95)

DESCRIPTION: The fun of this counting book lies in spotting the next thing to be counted ahead of time. As the determined hunter moves forward, he passes by cleverly camouflaged groups of animals until the end, when he sees them all—and makes a fast getaway.

COMMENTS: Spying the animals on the page before they show themselves is just the kind of reading and counting game preschoolers play over and over. Other peerless picks by this author include *Changes, Changes and *Rosie's Walk.

Roll Over (Mordicai Gerstein, Crown, 1988, 32 pp., $9.95)

DESCRIPTION: This story takes children from ten down to one, illustrating the concept of subtraction with child-level humor. As the little boy in the bed keeps telling the others to roll over, a variety of animals, like Sister Seal and Uncle Unicorn, fall out of bed, and the count goes down. The best part is that the pages are folded over so that the flap has to be lifted to see who has fallen out now.

COMMENTS: Another dynamic version of this counting song, with the same name, is by Merle Peek.

Ten Little Rabbits (Virginia Grossman and Sylvia Long, Chronicle, 1991, 26 pp., $12.95)

DESCRIPTION: From one rain dancer to ten sleepy weavers, this inspired counting book glows with Native American cultures and customs.

COMMENTS: A brief afterword describes American Indian traditions.

Fantasy and Humor

Young children have active imaginations and enjoy reading about magic and make-believe. They find humor in exaggeration, nonsense words, weird characters, and slapstick. The following stories, with silly situations and personification of animals and objects, tickle the funnybone, engage the imagination, and help clarify the differences between fact and fiction.

★Caps for Sale (Esphyr Slobodkina, HarperCollins, 1947, 48 pp., $10.95; (P) Trophy, 1987, $3.95)

DESCRIPTION: The hero is a peddler of caps who carries them all on his head. One day he falls asleep under a tree and wakes to find his wares on the heads of monkeys in a tree. How he gets them back is the charming ending of this story that has entertained generations.

COMMENTS: The repetitious language and action make this a prime candidate for dramatization. (Having lots of hats on hand will heighten the performance.)

The Cat in the Hat (Dr. Seuss, Random House, 1957, 72 pp., $6.95; (P) Random, 1987, $6.95)

DESCRIPTION: Two children with nothing to do sit and stare out at the rain. Suddenly, in walks an outrageous cat with some preposterous pranks. Fortunately, the fantastic feline has some tricks left when Mom reappears.

COMMENTS: Dr. Seuss will always be remembered for his more than 40 unforgettable stories and charismatic characters.

★Corduroy (Don Freeman, Viking, 1968, 32 pp., $11.95; (P) Puffin, 1988, $6.95)

DESCRIPTION: This story shows you don't have to be perfect to be loved. Children will fall for this sweet little bear (despite his one tiny flaw), as does the little girl who takes all the money from her piggy bank to buy him and bring him home.

COMMENTS: Other precious selections: *A Pocket for Corduroy, Mop Top,* and *Norman the Doorman.*

★Deep in the Forest (Brinton Turkle, Dutton, 1987, 32 pp., $12.95; (P) Dutton, 1976, $3.95)

DESCRIPTION: Goldilocks and the three bears is reversed in this tale-without-text of a cub who visits a cabin while the family is out. He eats the contents of Papa's, Mama's, and Baby's bowls, plays on their chairs, musses their beds, and is hiding under the covers in Baby's bed when the family comes home. The illustrations tell the story; readers supply the words.

COMMENTS: Comparing and contrasting this tale with the original *Goldilocks* expands critical-thinking skills.

Harold and the Purple Crayon (Crockett Johnson, HarperCollins, 1958, 64 pp., $10.95; (P) Trophy, 1981, $3.95)

DESCRIPTION: A small child goes for a moonlit walk with a remarkable crayon, and draws himself into and out of extraordinary escapades.

COMMENTS: Giving a preschooler a crayon, and letting imagination run wild, is a fitting culmination to this fantasy.

It Looked Like Spilt Milk (Charles G. Shaw, HarperCollins, 1947, 32 pp., $11.95; (P) Trophy, 1988, $3.95)

DESCRIPTION: An imagination-stretching book that will keep kids guessing until the very end, and encourage them to look at clouds with fresh eyes.

COMMENTS: Searching for new figures and forms in clouds follows naturally.

Jessica (Kevin Henkes, Greenwillow, 1989, 24 pp., $11.95; (P) Puffin, 1990, $3.95)

DESCRIPTION: Ruthie had a "pretend pal" who followed her everywhere. She even tagged along when Ruthie started kindergarten, where she was replaced by a real-life friend.

COMMENTS: Every child with an imaginary playmate will relate to this charmer.

Sheep in a Shop (Nancy Shaw, illustrated by Margot Apple, Houghton Mifflin, 1991, 32 pp., $12.95)

DESCRIPTION: The far-fetched fables of a fanciful flock and their forays (also in *Sheep in a Jeep* and *Sheep on a Ship*) are foolproof fleecy fun.

COMMENTS: The crisp rhyming language and bouncy beat will have lap-sitters chanting along in no time.

Where the Wild Things Are (Maurice Sendak, HarperCollins, 1988, 48 pp., $13.95; (P) Trophy, 1988, $4.95)

DESCRIPTION: Where else but in his dreams could Max sail away from his punishment for misbehaving? He went over the sea to where the wild things are, where he was "king," and no longer a helpless child. But Max was lonely, so he returned home—to his supper, and to where he was loved best of all.

COMMENTS: *The Nutshell Library* and *In the Night Kitchen* are just two more by the prestigious writer–illustrator of this Caldecott Medal winner.

Folktales

Folktales, passed down from generation to generation, please children with their rich, rhythmic language, cumulative word patterns, variety of subjects, and triumph of good over evil. Many fairy tales, however, contain frightening, violent themes for which young children are not yet ready. The following titles represent a blending of old and new treatments of traditional tales.

Anansi the Spider (Gerald McDermott, Holt, 1972, 40 pp., $14.95; (P) Holt, 1972, $5.95)

DESCRIPTION: Preschoolers may not grasp all the aspects of this rich Ashanti folktale. But the concepts of family caring and fair sharing will shine through. And, of course, they'll respond to the geometric graphics, the stylized plants and animals and the vibrant colors that capture the flavor of African designs and patterns.

COMMENTS: A Caldecott Honor Book.

Borreguita and the Coyote (Verna Aardema, illustrated by Petra Mathers, Knopf, 1991, 32 pp., $15)

DESCRIPTION: What's a little lamb to do about a fierce coyote that wants to eat her? In this fresh-as-springtime retelling of a Mexican folktale, she uses one clever trick after another to foil her foe.

COMMENTS: Comparing strategies used in this story with those of *The Three Pigs* and *The Billy Goats Gruff* aids thinking and reasoning skills.

The Fairy Tale Treasury (Virginia Haviland, illustrated by Raymond Briggs, Dell, 1986, 192 pp., $8.95)

DESCRIPTION: A comprehensive anthology of 32 tales, such as *The Gingerbread Boy, Henny Penny,* and *Jack and the Beanstalk,* gathered together for reading aloud to one or many.

COMMENTS: Two other recommended collections are *The Helen Oxenbury Nursery Story Book* and *Favorite Fairy Tales,* compiled by Edens and Darling.

Goldilocks and the Three Bears (James Marshall, Dial, 1988, 32 pp., $12.95)

DESCRIPTION: Old memories will come flooding back as readers introduce their children to Papa Bear, Mama Bear, and Baby Bear. But is the mind playing tricks? Was Goldilocks so naughty, was the dialogue so modern, and were the pictures so merry? Or is this the Caldecott Honor version that's not too hard, not too easy, but "just right?"

COMMENTS: Another simply wonderful version is by Byron
   Barton.

Little Red Riding Hood (John S. Goodall, McElderry, 1988, 32
pp., $14.95)

DESCRIPTION: They're all here—Little Red Riding Hood,
   grandma, the wicked wolf, and the woodcutter. But in this
   fresh interpretation, there are no words, the heroine is a
   mouse, and the villain is all dressed up in top hat. Despite
   these whimsical changes, it all ends happily (of course) with an
   old-fashioned tea party.

COMMENTS: The half-pages to turn—the author's trade-
   mark—add variety and interest to the tale.

The Three Billy Goats Gruff (P. C. Asbjornsen and J. E. Moe,
illustrated by Marcia Brown, (P) Harcourt Brace Jovanovich,
1991, $3.95)

DESCRIPTION: This folktale of courage and strategy tells of
   how three smart Billy Goats outwit the mean troll, then live
   happily ever after eating grass on a sunny hillside.

COMMENTS: Voice modulation (for the different-sized goats)
   and refrains inviting participation (Trip, trap, trip, trap) are
   surefire storytelling techniques.

The Three Little Pigs (Margot Zemach, (P) Farrar, Straus &
Giroux, 1991, $3.95)

DESCRIPTION: Here are some of the best-known words in
   children's literature: "Little pig, little pig, let me come in. No,
   no, not by the hair of my chinny-chin-chin. Then I'll huff and
   I'll puff and I'll blow your house down."

COMMENTS: In this and other traditional tellings, the pigs and wolf are eaten, so parents must judge for themselves if their preschoolers are ready.

Independence and Achievement

As children grow and develop, they experiment with newly acquired skills. Although generally eager to become more independent, they are occasionally ambivalent and need the reassurance of a loving figure. Stories about achievement illustrate the power of persistence and the pride of purpose. The following classics with themes of "dependence/independence" and "overcoming seemingly insurmountable odds" have a special appeal to us all.

★The Carrot Seed (Ruth Krauss, HarperCollins, 1945, 24 pp., $10.95; (P) Trophy, 1989, $3.95)

DESCRIPTION: This simple story makes it clear that it's okay to stick by what you believe in, even if others tell you it won't work. With a little work and patience, it just might.

COMMENTS: Planting seeds and watching them grow are great learning experiences.

★The Little Engine That Could (Watty Piper, illustrated by George and Doris Hauman, Platt and Munk, 1990, 48 pp., $12.95)

DESCRIPTION: In a world where children often feel small and powerless, like the toys on the train, they'll see that being small doesn't matter if you believe in yourself like the little engine.

COMMENTS: The well-known refrain "I think I can, I think I can" points up the power of positive thinking for both children and adults.

★*Mike Mulligan and His Steam Shovel* (Virginia Lee Burton, Houghton Mifflin, 1939, 48 pp., $11.95; (P) Houghton Mifflin, 1939, $4.95)

DESCRIPTION: Mike and Mary Ann, his steam shovel, dig a cellar for the city hall in just one day in an unusual story of love, loyalty, and faith.

COMMENTS: *The Little House* and *Katy and the Big Snow* are other memorable works by this author.

★*The Runaway Bunny* (Margaret Wise Brown, illustrated by Clement Hurd, HarperCollins, 1942, 40 pp., $11.95; (P) Trophy, 1977, $3.95)

DESCRIPTION: When this little bunny tells his mother he's running away, she lets him know that no matter where he goes or what he becomes she's going to be right there too, because he's her little bunny. If he joins the circus as a trapeze artist, she'll be on the high wire walking across the air to get him. If he becomes a little boy and runs into a house, she'll be the mother waiting to take him in her arms and hug him.

COMMENTS: Children need the reassurance that parents will always be there "no matter what."

★*The Story about Ping* (Marjorie Flack, illustrated by Kurt Wiese, Viking, 1933, 32 pp., $11.95; (P) Penguin, 1989, $6.95)

DESCRIPTION: Poor Ping! Rather than be spanked for being the last duck on the boat, he hides. But in the morning his boat is gone, and he suffers some nervous moments before he's finally reunited with his family.

COMMENTS: This tale expresses separation anxiety sometimes felt when experimenting with independence; the happy ending is comforting.

★The Tale of Peter Rabbit (Beatrix Potter, Warner, 1902, 1989, 58 pp., $8.95; (P) Crown, 1988, $2.50)

DESCRIPTION: An all-time best seller that continues to charm both children and adults, no matter how many times it's read. Mischievous Peter's narrow escape from farmer McGregor is just the beginning of the many adventures of this sweet, very human little bunny.

COMMENTS: This classic tale unerringly portrays themes of exploration and independence.

★When You Were a Baby (Ann Jonas, Greenwillow, 1982, 24 pp., $14.95; (P) Puffin, 1986, $3.95)

DESCRIPTION: Children can celebrate all the wonderful things they can do now that they're no longer babies. Like drinking from a glass, rolling a ball, taking kitty for a ride, and so many other things that make both parent and child proud.

COMMENTS: Kids love to hear their "baby stories." Realizing how much they've mastered imbues confidence for new challenges.

Poetry and Rhymes

Children have a natural love of rhythm and rhyme, and they respond to poems of all sorts. Mother Goose and nursery rhymes, often a child's first exposure to poetry, provide imaginative use of words, variety of verse, and madcap nonsense. The titles below represent a sampling of some of the choicest contemporary and traditional poems around.

A Cup of Starshine: Poems and Pictures for Young Children (Jill Bennett, illustrated by Graham Percy, Harcourt Brace Jovanovich, 1991, 64 pp., $16.95)

DESCRIPTION: A diverse anthology that's perfect for giving young children their first delicious taste of poetry. Verses about the ordinary and the amazing offer new ways of experimenting with sounds and seeing the world.

COMMENTS: Includes such well-known poets as Margaret Wise Brown, Eleanor Farjeon, and Lee Bennett Hopkins.

The Eentsy, Weentsy Spider: Fingerplays and Action Rhymes (Joanna Cole and Stephanie Calmenson, illustrated by Alan Tiegreen, Morrow, 1991, 64 pp., $13.95)

DESCRIPTION: These entertaining, easy-to-remember rhymes and finger games, a mainstay of child care and nursery programs for years, are accompanied by pictures with directional arrows to demonstrate the right motions for each poem. Scores are provided at the end for musical accompaniment.

COMMENTS: *Hand Rhymes* by Marc Brown is another highly recommended book of the same genre.

Fathers, Mothers, Sisters, Brothers (Mary Ann Hoberman, illustrated by Marylin Hafner, Little, Brown, 1991, 32 pp., $14.95)

DESCRIPTION: Wry rhymes about home and family (cozy cousins, indulgent grandparents) are combined with more serious subjects, such as relationships (fighting with siblings), feelings (shyness with strangers), adoption, and divorce.

COMMENTS: Other works by the author are *A House Is a House for Me* and *The Cozy Book.*

The Little Dog Laughed and Other Nursery Rhymes (Lucy Cousins, Dutton, 1990, 64 pp., $14.95)

DESCRIPTION: In this fast-paced, zippy treatment of 64 traditional rhymes, the brilliant colors leap out, the droll illustrations tickle, and the just-right, childlike letters in the titles infuse new life into the old favorites.

COMMENTS: *What Can Robbit See?* and *What Can Rabbit Hear?* are sturdy board books with tempting flaps to lift.

Michael Foreman's Mother Goose (Michael Foreman, Harcourt Brace Jovanovich, 1991, 160 pp., $19.95)

DESCRIPTION: An artistically exquisite collection of more than 200 nursery rhymes with visual links connecting the pages. When Mary Mary quite contrary works in her garden, two legs are seen dangling mysteriously, and on the next page, readers realize that they belong to the now-fallen Humpty Dumpty.

COMMENTS: Wonderful recent Mother Goose editions also include those by Tomie de Paola, Arnold Lobel, and Wendy Watson.

Read-Aloud Rhymes for the Very Young (Jack Prelutsky, illustrated by Marc Brown, Knopf, 1986, 112 pp., $15.95)

DESCRIPTION: These sparkling 200+ poems range from animals ("The Little Turtle") to activities ("Jump or Jiggle"), fantasy ("I Can Be a Tiger") to feelings ("Joyful"), manners ("Table Manners") to mayhem ("Somersaults").

COMMENTS: Other books by this master poet and anthologist include *The Random House Book of Poetry for Children* and *Poems of a Nonny Mouse.*

Sing a Song of Popcorn: Every Child's Book of Poems (Beatrice de Regniers and others, Scholastic, 1988, 142 pp., $18.95)

DESCRIPTION: Culled from works of renowned poets, these 128 great selections are grouped by such themes as weather, animals, people, nonsense, and feelings.

COMMENTS: Illustrations are in full color by nine Caldecott Medal-winning artists.

Talking Like the Rain: A First Book of Poems (X. J. Kennedy and Dorothy M. Kennedy, illustrated by Jane Dyer, Little, Brown, 1992, 96 pp., $17.95)

DESCRIPTION: Compiled especially for the youngest child, this rainbow of more than 100 poems is by turns playful, funny, mischievous, and thoughtful.

COMMENTS: Includes poems by Edward Lear, Christina Rossetti, Robert Louis Stevenson, and many newer voices.

The Tall Book of Mother Goose (Feodor Rojankovsy, Harper-Collins, 1942, 120 pp., $7.95)

DESCRIPTION: It's not just the shape of this Mother Goose book that has made it such a hit for the past 50 years. It's also the presentation, pictures, and the feeling of fun that flows from the pages.

COMMENTS: Among the multitude of Mother Goose notables: *Book of Nursery and Mother Goose Rhymes*—De Angeli, *Mother Goose*—Voland Edition, and *The Real Mother Goose*—Wright.

School

Children are starting school at younger ages than ever before. Many 3- and 4-year-olds attend preschool programs; increasing numbers of infants and toddlers are being placed in child care settings by working parents. Separating from home and family, and adjusting to new situations, can cause feelings of stress and anxiety. Nancy Balaban, a noted educator, feels that it's important for parents and children to plan for these parting experiences and to share their feelings about them.[2] The following stories prepare young children for day care, nursery school, or kindergarten.

Going to Day Care (Fred Rogers, Putnam, 1985, 32 pp., $12.95; (P) Putnam, 1985, $5.95)

DESCRIPTION: A candid discussion of day care, with large, full-color photographs, explaining what it's like and what to expect. Questions in the text, such as "How do you feel when mom or dad has to leave you for a while," encourage open communication.

COMMENTS: The star of children's televison offers advice on how to cope with preschool problems of *Going to the: Potty, Doctor, Hospital; When a Pet Dies,* and *Moving.*

Going to My Nursery School (Susan Kuklin, Bradbury, 1990, 40 pp., $12.95)

DESCRIPTION: Father takes 4-year-old Heath to meet his teacher and see the class in a photojournal tour of nursery school. The text details the daily routines; the close-ups record the children's accomplishments, enthusiasms, and temporary worries. The final page provides tips to parents on what to look for in a nursery school.

COMMENTS: Others that address preschool concerns are *When I See My Dentist* and *When I See My Doctor.*

I Don't Want To (Sally Grindley, illustrated by Sally Thompson, Little, Brown, 1990, 28 pp., $13.95)

DESCRIPTION: Jim doesn't want to put on his clothes, eat his breakfast, and, most of all, go to nursery school. When he gets there, he refuses to join in but later succumbs when he sees how much fun the others are having. And, of course, when it's time to go home, he doesn't want to.

COMMENTS: A reassuring look at nursery school.

Maybe She Forgot (Ellen Kandoian, Dutton, 1990, 32 pp., $12.95)

DESCRIPTION: Jessie has just spent her first day at dance class and it's time to go home. One by one all the other children are picked up, until Jessie, left waiting all alone, begins to cry. The reader can see that Mom is delayed by traffic and a flat tire but finally rushes in to lovingly assure Jessie, "I could never forget about you."

COMMENTS: This simple, charming story eloquently expresses the fear of abandonment common to young children.

My Nursery School (Harlow Rockwell, (P) Mulberry, 1990, 32 pp., $3.95)

DESCRIPTION: Warmly colored illustrations of nursery niceties—books and blocks, paint and puzzles, even guppies and a hamster—engender eagerness to attend.

COMMENTS: Other books to prepare youngsters for potentially upsetting experiences are *My Dentist* and *My Doctor.*

Starting School (Janet and Allen Ahlberg, (P) Puffin, 1990, 32 pp., $3.95)

DESCRIPTION: This hospitable introduction to nursery school helps calm preschool jitters by acquainting children with the teacher, classroom, fun-to-do activities, and soon-to-be new friends.

COMMENTS: The authors have many wonderful books to their credit: *Each Peach Pear Plum, The Jolly Postman, The Jolly Christmas Postman,* and *Peek-a-Boo.*

★*Will I Have a Friend?* (Miriam Cohen, illustrated by Lillian Hoban, Macmillan, 1967, 32 pp., $12.95; (P) Aladdin, 1989, $3.95)

DESCRIPTION: A time-honored treatment of fears of starting school and finding friends. Jim worries, "Will I have a friend?" and feels left out and all alone until he meets Paul.

COMMENTS: Jim and Paul's friendship continues in *The New Teacher, When Will I Read?* and *Best Friends.*

Nature

Books can draw attention to the wonder and beauty of nature and to concepts of growth, change, and time. The following books are ideal to help young children learn about weather, the seasons, natural events, and living things.

Caps, Hats, Socks, and Mittens (Louise Borden, illustrated by Lillian Hoban, (P) Scholastic, 1992, 32 pp., $3.95)

DESCRIPTION: This book highlights scenes and sensations of the four seasons and the fun to be had at any time of year.

COMMENTS: Discussing favorite seasonal activities are timely topics that promote verbal expression.

Dawn (Uri Shulevitz, Farrar, Straus & Giroux, 1974, 32 pp., $14.95; (P) Farrar, 1988, $4.95)

DESCRIPTION: As dawn approaches, an old man and his grandson ride out onto a lake in their boat. Poetic images, with changing shades and hues, symbolize the serenity of night easing into morning, and the daily wonder of new beginnings.

COMMENTS: This lyrical Caldecott Medal winner was inspired by an ancient Chinese poem.

Gilberto and the Wind (Marie Hall Ets, Viking, 1963, 32 pp., $12.95, (P) Puffin, 1978, $3.95)

DESCRIPTION: The sound of the wind beckons a small boy to come out and play. As they race, fly kites, and have fun together, Gilberto learns how the wind can be gentle, playful, and helpful, but also powerful and a little scary.

COMMENTS: Other well-seasoned titles: *In the Forest* and *Play with Me.*

★Peter Spier's Rain (Peter Spier, Doubleday, 1982, 40 pp., $12.95; (P) Doubleday, 1987, $6.95)

DESCRIPTION: A brother and sister, safeguarded in raingear, splash and sport in this all-picture showery scenario.

COMMENTS: *Crash! Bang! Boom!* and *Gobble Growl Grunt* are both about sounds; *Noah's Ark* is a Caldecott Medal winner.

★The Snowy Day (Ezra Jack Keats, (P) Puffin, 1976, 32 pp., $3.95)

DESCRIPTION: So much to do in the newly fallen snow—make tracks, snowballs, angels, and smiling snowmen—as a small boy frolics in a world of winter white.

COMMENTS: The same dear boy of this Caldecott Medal winner stars in *Peter's Chair* and *Whistle for Willie.*

A Tree Is Nice (Janice M. Udry, illustrated by Marc Simont, HarperCollins, 1957, 32 pp., $11.95)

DESCRIPTION: Delights to be had in, with, or under trees depict their beauty and importance.

COMMENTS: Follow-ups can include observing, discussing, drawing, and writing about trees.

Vegetable Garden (Douglas Florian, Harcourt Brace Jovanovich, 1991, 32 pp., $13.95)

DESCRIPTION: With simple rhyming text and bold, colorful illustrations, this book instructs young gardeners as they watch a family plant, tend, and harvest a vegetable garden.

COMMENTS: A logical lead-in for learning about different kinds of vegetables.

★The Very Hungry Caterpillar (Eric Carle, Putnam, 1981, 28 pp., $15.95)

DESCRIPTION: A little caterpillar who eats his way through apples, oranges, pickles, pie, a lollipop, and more builds a cocoon, and emerges as a beautiful butterfly. This book is extraspecial fun thanks to the real hole that has attracted millions of young fingers worldwide.

COMMENTS: Other very good "Very" books are *The Very Busy Spider, The Very Hungry Cat,* and *The Very Quiet Cricket.*

Things That Go

Preschoolers are fascinated by "things that move" and "how things work." The following books about diverse forms of transportation and machines increase knowledge and awareness of the world.

Bikes (Anne Rockwell, Dutton, (P) 1987, 24 pp., $3.95)

DESCRIPTION: Driven by tiger-children, bikes of every shape and variety, including tricycles, unicycles, and mopeds, wheel on by.

COMMENTS: Also in the author's fleet of transportation books are *Boats, Cars, Fire Engines,* and *Planes.*

★*Freight Train* (Donald Crews, Greenwillow, 1978, 32 pp., $13.95; (P) Puffin, 1985, $3.95)

DESCRIPTION: From the caboose to the steam engine, the cars are named at a pace that mimics a train barely moving from a station. The whole train starts to gather speed as colorful cars blur past cities, over trestles, and onward.

COMMENTS: Besides this Caldecott Honor Book, this versatile author has written many excellent books in the same and other genres.

Machines at Work (Byron Barton, Crowell, 1987, 32 pp., $7.95)

DESCRIPTION: Easy, limited text and vivid drawings supply a snapshot of a construction site. Men and women use all kinds of machines—cranes, steam rollers, bulldozers—to lift beams, build roads, and put up a building.

COMMENTS: Visits to places of interest in the neighborhood expand language and learning.

Richard Scarry's Cars and Trucks and Things That Go (Richard Scarry, Golden, 1974, 69 pp., $10.95)

DESCRIPTION: Powered by a sense of humor and almost human animals, this very busy transportation travelogue is packed with all kinds of vehicles that'll keep kids absorbed for hours.

COMMENTS: This author's information-packed books have helped toddlers learn about words, nursery rhymes, people, and more.

Tools (Venice Shone, Scholastic, 1991, 28 pp., $9.95)

DESCRIPTION: Tools for cutting, joining, measuring, painting, decorating, gardening, and also cleaning up when the work is done are prettily presented and neatly labeled. A glossary explains their uses and how they work.

COMMENTS: Children should be cautioned that many tools are heavy or sharp, and should be handled only by adults.

Truck Song (Diane Siebert, illustrated by Byron Barton, Crowell, 1984, 32 pp., $13.95; (P) Trophy, 1987, $4.95)

DESCRIPTION: "Armored trucks that carry cash, garbage trucks that carry trash." Rhymes such as these capture the rhythmic motion of a cross-country trip, with all kinds of trucks in all kinds of places in all kinds of weather.

COMMENTS: Bold, striking illustrations accentuate this tribute to trucks and truckers (and to the little kids who love them).

The Wheels on the Bus (Paul O. Zelinsky, Dutton, 1990, 12 pp., $14.95)

DESCRIPTION: The pull-tabs in this "motion" picture book put little kids in the driver's seat, making the doors open and shut, the wipers swish, and the riders go bumpity-bump.

COMMENTS: Hand and body movements are great rhythmic accompaniments to this well-known verse.

FREE OR INEXPENSIVE MATERIALS

The following sources provide valuable information either free of charge or at minimal cost.

The Boston Globe, P.O. Box 2378, Boston, MA 02107-2378.

The Young Reader. A quarterly newsletter that fosters children's reading with practical advice and recommended books. Free with stamped, self-addressed, business-size envelope.

Center for the Study of Reading, 51 Gerty Drive, Champaign, IL 61820, 217-933-2552.

Ten Ways to Help Your Children Become Better Readers. Suggestions on helping and encouraging children at home. Sample copy is free.

The Children's Book Council, Order Center, 350 Scotland Road, Orange, NJ 07050-2398, 800-666-7608.

Choosing a Child's Book. Basic points about finding the right books for babies to children age 12 and up, and an annotated list of resources. Sample copy is free; 25 copies are $15.

Consumer Information Catalogue, R. Woods, Consumer Information Center-Y, P.O. Box 100, Pueblo, CO 81002. Make checks payable to "Superintendent of Documents."

Becoming a Nation of Readers: What Parents Can Do (447X). Activities and techniques to help children build skills. 50¢.
Books for Children (139X). Descriptions of the best recent books from preschool through junior high. $1.
Help Your Child Become a Good Reader (449X). Suggestions to teach reading fundamentals that center around everyday occurrences and items. 50¢.
Help Your Child Learn to Write Well (453X). Strategies to help beginning writers express their ideas. 50¢.
Helping Your Child Use the Library (455X). Tips on getting children of all ages, including those with special needs, interested in books. 50¢.
Summertime Favorites (456X). Nearly 400 literature classics published before 1960 for children of all ages. 50¢.

International Reading Association, 800 Barksdale Road, P.O. Box 8139, Newark, DE 19714-8139, 800-336-7323, Fax: 302-731-1057. The brochures below focus on practical concerns of parents and on developing children's lifetime reading habits. Single copies are free with a business-size, stamped, self-addressed envelope; 100 copies are $6.50. Requests for four to six brochures must be accompanied by first-class postage for two ounces.

Good Books Make Reading Fun for Your Child, Glenna Davis Sloan. (Also available in French)

Summer Reading Is Important, John Micklos, Jr. (French also)

You Can Encourage Your Child to Read (French and Spanish also)

You Can Help Your Child Connect Reading to Writing, Nicholas P. Criscuolo.

You Can Use Television to Stimulate Your Child's Reading Habits, Nicholas P. Criscuolo. (French and Spanish also)

Your Home Is Your Child's First School (French and Spanish also)

The series of 16- to 24-page booklets that follow focus on answering questions parents often ask about the education of their children. 1–24 copies are $1.75 each; 25–99 copies are $1.50 each; 100+ copies are $1.25 each.

Children's Choices. A booklist of newly published books chosen by children as their favorites sponsored jointly by the International Reading Association and the Children's Book Council. Books selected have been grouped by reading levels with annotations and bibliographic data. Single copies are free with a self-addressed 9" × 12" envelope with four ounce, first-class postage; 10 copies are $4.25; 100 copies are $35.

Helping Your Child Become a Reader (#161), Nancy L. Roser. Suggestions for parental involvement in children's learning.

How Can I Prepare My Young Child for Reading? (#163), Paula C. Grinnel. Parents' roles as their child's first teachers in the critical educational years from birth through kindergarten.

You Can Help Your Young Child with Writing (#160), Marcia

Baghban. How parents can help by giving encouragement and support to their children as they learn to write by writing.

National Association for the Education of Young Children, 1834 Connecticut Avenue, N.W., Washington, DC 20009-5786, 800-424-2460, Fax: 202-328-1846. Single copies of the following are 50¢; 100 copies are $10.

African American Literature for Young Children (#568). A child resource list, developed by the National Black Child Development Institute, of children's books that provide accurate and realistic images of black people and reinforce the importance of African American cultural traditions.

Helping Children Learn about Reading (#520), J. A. Schickedanz. How to make learning to read a meaningful part of lives of infants, toddlers, and preschoolers.

Los niños pequeños (preescolares a tercer grado): Desarrollo de la lectura y de la expresión oral y escrita (#521). Spanish edition of a joint statement prepared by the Early Childhood and Literacy Development Committee of the International Reading Association expressing concerns and providing recommendations for improving practices related to literacy development.

The National PTA, 700 North Rush Street, Chicago, IL 60611-2571, 312-787-0977, Fax: 312-787-8342.

Help Your Child Become a Good Reader (B-323). Ideas to help children ages 3 to 6 become good readers. Contains tips for making reading activities fun, understanding the connection between reading and writing, and choosing books children will like. Single copies are free with a business-size, self-addressed, stamped envelope; 50 copies are $6; 100 copies are $10.

Reading Is Fundamental, Inc., Publications Department, 600 Maryland Avenue, S.W., Suite 500, Washington, DC 20024, 202-287-3220, Fax: 202-287-3196.

Building a Family Library. Ideas for creating an inexpensive home library and helping children build their own collections. Single copy is 50¢; 100 copies are $20.

Children's Bookshelf. An annotated list of 106 books organized for four age ranges; Infancy–3, 3–5, 5–8, 8–11. Single copy is $1; 100 copies are $25.

Choosing Good Books for Children. Information and resources to help parents find appropriate books for their children from infancy to age 12. 50¢.

Encouraging Soon-to-Be Readers. How to excite preschoolers about books and help them to develop the skills that lead to reading. 50¢.

Encouraging Young Writers. Activities that motivate preschoolers to begin writing and school-age children to write more. 50¢.

Family Storytelling. Tips and techniques for telling stories, and turning to books for more. 50¢.

Magazines and Family Reading. Ways that magazines can get the whole family turning pages. 50¢.

Reading Aloud to Your Children. The why's, when's, where's, what's, and how's of reading aloud. 50¢.

Reading Is Fun! Simple ways parents can prepare their young children for reading and help them along as they begin to read on their own. Single copies are $1; 100 copies are $30.

TV and Reading. Suggestions to help parents help their children achieve a healthy balance. 50¢.

Upbeat and Offbeat Activities to Encourage Reading. Playful projects and activities to help preschoolers and beginning readers build skills. 50¢.

When We Were Young: Favorite Books of RIF Kids, RIF Volunteers, and Readers of Renown. A list of all-time favorite children's books and others considered "too good to miss." Also includes the personal recommendations and encouragement of approximately 80 celebrated public figures, such as Ronald Reagan, Barbara Walters, and Erma Bombeck. 75¢.

Chapter 3

Book Clubs

KEVIN ATKINSON

Almost everyone is familiar with book clubs for adults. Less well known, however, is the number of book clubs available for young children. These clubs deal in a wide variety of literature. Some focus on familiar cartoon or TV characters; others are geared to school, rather than home, distribution. Benefits include the choice of preselected, quality books, discounted prices, convenient home delivery, and personally addressed packages (which kids love). Clubs are also a great way to build a library and start the reading habit early.

Book clubs generally offer incentives to join, such as reduced prices and/or gifts, such as T-shirts, book racks, or tote bags. Then the clubs take two forms. One type automatically mails out the books, which can be kept or returned within a specified time period. The second type sends newsletters describing the books, and parents and children make their own selections. Depending upon the club, subscribers can cancel either at any time or after satisfying an initial enrollment agreement. Shipping and handling charges, and applicable sales tax, are additional. Recent introductory offers are provided as examples, but since these and other specifics are subject to change, it's a good idea to call for the latest information.

HOME BOOK CLUBS

Book-of-the-Month Club
Customer Service Center
Camp Hill, PA 17012-8801
800-233-1066

Books of My Very Own (Four age groups: Baby books: 6 months–2 years (board books, pop-ups, sturdy paperbacks); Picture books: 2–4 years; Storybooks: 4–7 years; Adventures, Mysteries, Puzzles, Games: 7–10 years)

DESCRIPTION: *Introductory offer:* 3 books and T-shirt for $5.95. *Description:* About every 5 weeks, a package of 3 to 4 books is mailed automatically on approval, with option to purchase or return within 10 days. *Price:* $13.95 per package. *Commitment:* No obligation to buy; membership can be canceled at any time.

COMMENTS: Package includes mix of hard- and softcover books from a variety of publishers. Age groupings can be changed easily as child matures.

Children's Book-of-the-Month Club (Same age groups as **Books of My Very Own**)

DESCRIPTION: *Introductory offer:* 3 books and tote bag for $3. *Description:* 15 times a year, about every 3½ weeks, a book review is mailed to the home. Recommended selection for indicated age group will be sent automatically unless an alternative or no book is indicated. *Price:* Generally range from $8.95 to $14.95. *Commitment:* 3 books within one year of enrollment.

COMMENTS: Review features 40 books for children from babies to preteens plus games and contests.

Doubleday Children's Book Club (6550 East 30th Street, P.O. Box 6325, Indianapolis, IN 46206-6325, 800-688-4442; Two age groups: under 5 years, over 5 years)

DESCRIPTION: *Introductory offer:* Children's Picture Dictionary and 3 books for $3. *Description:* A monthly magazine describing books is mailed to the home; parent (and child) decide on selections. *Price:* Generally range from $8 to $11 per book. *Commitment:* 4 books within one year of enrollment.

COMMENTS: Offering magazine features special activity games, such as coloring contests and puzzles, for participation fun.

Field Publications
4343 Equity Drive
Columbus, OH 43228
800-999-7100

This company has an assortment of book clubs for varying ages and interests. The ones that follow are appropriate for preschoolers.

Disney Babies Learn About Series (Ages 1–3)

DESCRIPTION: *Introductory offer:* 3 books, 2 activity books, and bookcase free; 1 book on approval, with option to purchase or return within 14 days. *Description:* 2 books sent monthly on 14-day approval. *Price:* $3.99 per book. *Commitment:* 3 shipments of 2 books each.

COMMENTS: Selections feature baby Disney characters geared to beginning learning. They are all board books with sturdy pages and rounded (nonsharp) corners specifically sized (6″ × 7″) for small fingers.

I Can Read Book Club (Ages 3–8)

DESCRIPTION: *Introductory offer:* 6 books for 25¢; 2 books on 14-day approval. *Description:* 2 books sent on 14-day approval every 5–6 weeks. *Price:* $4.49 per book. *Commitment:* 3 shipments of 2 books each.

COMMENTS: Books are from Harper & Row's *I Can Read* series by celebrated authors and illustrators designed for beginning readers (short sentences, easy vocabulary).

Weekly Reader Book Club (Primary Division, ages 4–7)

DESCRIPTION: *Introductory offer:* 8 books for $3.99. *Description:* 2 books sent on 14-day approval every 5–6 weeks. *Price:* $4.99 per book. *Commitment:* 3 shipments of 2 books each.

COMMENTS: Contemporary and classic hardcover picture books with focus on variety.

Magic Castle Readers (Ages 2–5)

DESCRIPTION: *Introductory offer:* Free book, poster, stickers, Parents' Guide, and 1 book on approval, with option to purchase or return within 14 days. *Description:* 2 more shipments of 2 books each sent on approval at 6-week intervals. Remaining 21 books are sent on approval in single shipment. *Price:* $5.99 each initial book; complete 21-book package approximately $150, including shipping and handling, payable in monthly installments.

COMMENTS: 32-page, 9″ × 8″ hardcover books, written by Jane Moncure, cover such early-learning concepts as numbers, colors, rhyming, and key words.

Just Ask Series (Ages 4–7)

DESCRIPTION: *Introductory offer:* Free book and Legos; 1 book on approval with option to purchase or return within 14 days. *Description:* 2 more shipments of 2 books each sent on approval at 6-week intervals. Remaining 26 books sent on approval in single shipment (with free book box and set of marker pens). *Price:* $4.99 each initial book; complete 26-book shipment approximately $135, including shipping and handling, payable in monthly installments.

COMMENTS: These hardcover books introduce early science and nature concepts.

Golden Press
Western Publishing Company
120 Brighton Road
Clifton, NJ 07012-9805
800-537-1517

Sesame Street Book Club (Ages 2–6)

DESCRIPTION: *Introductory offer:* 1 book and Sesame Street Alphabet and Numbers Flash Cards free; 2 books on approval, with option to purchase or return within 14 days. *Description:* 2 books are sent monthly on approval. *Price:* $4.29 per book. *Commitment:* No obligation to buy; membership can be canceled at any time.

COMMENTS: Hardcover books, which feature the Sesame Street characters, help children learn skills within a story format.

Big Bird Beep Books (Ages 2–6)

DESCRIPTION: *Introductory offer:* Big Bird Beep Book of ABC's, Answer Finder, and Sesame Street Grow Chart for $1. *Descrip-*

tion: 2 books sent monthly on approval, with option to purchase or return within 14 days. *Price:* $4.49 per book. *Commitment:* No obligation to buy; membership can be canceled at any time.

COMMENTS: Featuring the Sesame Street characters, the books focus on teaching basic skills, such as the alphabet, counting, colors, and shapes. They contain questions and answers, treated with special, safety-tested ink, that beep upon contact with the Big Bird Answer Finder. Books are softcover and spiral bound.

Grolier Enterprises
Sherman Turnpike
Danbury, CT 06816
203-797-3500
800-955-9877

Grolier has many different book programs for children of all ages, as evidenced by the sampling below. Generally, shipments of 2 books are mailed monthly, although there are a variety of offers and terms. They suggest calling their toll-free number for specific information regarding introductory offers, pricing, and cancellation policies.

Beginning Readers' Program: Dr. Seuss and His Friends (Ages 1–4)

DESCRIPTION: Easy-to-read storybooks featuring Dr. Seuss favorites, the Berenstain Bears, and other picture books.

COMMENTS: 72-title series.

Disney's Wonderful World of Reading (Ages 1–4)

DESCRIPTION: Picture-book adventures featuring Mickey and Minnie Mouse, Donald Duck, and other Disney characters.

COMMENTS: 150-title series.

Muppet Babies Good Start Library (Ages 2–5)

DESCRIPTION: Jim Henson's Muppet Babies teach early learning concepts, and explore such experiences as bedtime and going to the doctor.

COMMENTS: 24-book series.

Alphapets (Ages 3–7)

DESCRIPTION: Picture books in which 26 animal characters personifying particular characteristics or traits reinforce letter recognition while teaching the importance of worthwhile behavior.

COMMENTS: A series of 30 books.

Hello Reading (Ages 3–7)

DESCRIPTION: Easy readers that use repetition and simple text to progressively build reading skills.

COMMENTS: 30 stories by respected children's author Harriet Ziefert.

Young Readers Book Club (Ages 3–7)

DESCRIPTION: Books to provide reading pleasure from a variety of publishers and well-known authors and illustrators.

COMMENTS: 28-title program by such writers as Marc Brown, Cynthia Rylant, Charlotte Zolotow, and others.

In the following programs, initial books are mailed monthly; then remaining titles are sent in a single shipment, payable in monthly installments.

My First Steps to Reading (Ages 0–3)

DESCRIPTION: Books that explore the world of words and the alphabet for the very young.

COMMENTS: 25-title program comes with word cards for each letter for optional use.

My First Steps to Math (Ages 1–6)

DESCRIPTION: Series to help children learn about numbers and build early math skills.

COMMENTS: 10-book program.

Help Me Be Good (Ages 2–5)

DESCRIPTION: Program that explores and teaches kids how to deal effectively with such problems as teasing, lying, selfishness, and anger.

COMMENTS: 29 books written by developmentalist Joy Berry.

Alice in Bibleland (Ages 2–6)

DESCRIPTION: Well-known stories to promote an early understanding of the Bible, and to encourage a pleasurable view of reading.

COMMENTS: 24 books are in verse form.

Getting to Know Nature's Children (Ages 3–7)

DESCRIPTION: Stories of nature and animal life with colorful photos and easy text.

COMMENTS: 26-book series.

Parents Magazine Read Aloud Book Club (1 Parents Circle, P.O. Box 10264, Des Moines, IA 50336-0264, 800-678-5660; Ages 6 months–4 years)

DESCRIPTION: *Introductory offer:* 2 books, growth chart, book rack, and tote bag free; 2 books on approval with option to purchase or return within 14 days. *Description:* 2 books are sent monthly on approval. *Price:* $4.29 per book. *Commitment:* No obligation to buy; membership can be canceled at any time.

COMMENTS: Hardcover books are by well-known children's authors and illustrators created especially for *Parents Magazine.* "From Parents to Parents," a newsletter included with each shipment, contains suggestions and ideas. A "Clown-Arounds' Activity Page," another regular feature, provides activities for youngsters. Bonus stamps, earned when shipments are kept, are good toward a free Bonus Book selection.

SCHOOL BOOK CLUBS

The following book clubs are geared to group distribution, such as school, day-care, and religious settings. Teachers receive monthly offerings (September through June), which are sent home, of a wide selection of hard- and softcovered books, generally ranging in price from $.50 to $3.95. Some audio- and videocassettes are also included. Parent indicates choices and returns to teacher with payment. There is no obligation for either teacher or parent to buy at any time. Teachers earn bonus points with each order toward free books or enrichment materials. Minimum class order is $10 or 10 paid items; postage, shipping, and handling charges are paid by the company.

Carnival Book Clubs, P.O. Box 6035, Columbia, MO 65205-6035, 800-654-3037. Kindergarten through grade two edition.

Scholastic Book Clubs, 2391 E. McCarty Street, P.O. Box 7500, Jefferson City, MO 65102-9981, 800-325-6149. Book clubs for preschoolers through grade nine. *Firefly* is the preschool edition; *See Saw* is for kindergarten and grade one.

Troll Book Clubs, 2 Lethbridge Plaza, Mahwah, NJ 07430, 800-541-1097. Book clubs for preschoolers through grade nine. There is one edition for pre-kindergarten and kindergarten; another for kindergarten and grade one.

Chapter 4

Computer Software

Computers have been touted as the greatest educational tool since chalk—a must for the classroom, a boon for the home.[1] Hype or hope? At this point, the research is inconclusive. What is certain, however, is that computers have become an integral part of our lives and that children are being exposed to, and using, them at younger ages than ever before. This has raised some questions and concerns. Are computers beneficial for young children? At what age should children be introduced to the computer? Should parents buy one for their preschooler?

COMPUTER COMPLIMENTS

Educators recognize the value and versatility of computers. The Southern Early Childhood Association believes that computers can broaden literacy, strengthen play, and enhance art, music, and problem-solving experiences.[2] Computers are also patient (particularly valuable for young children), nonjudgmental, and promote self-assurance in handling technology.[3] They afford opportunities for shared "quality time" experiences and, with their fascinating graphics, animation, colors, and sounds, can make learning great fun!

Not everyone is quite so enthusiastic. Some experts caution that computers must be used on a playful and limited basis and be suited to the child's level of development.[4] However, like it or not, computers are here to stay, and the challenge is to use them appropriately and effectively.

GOOD BEGINNINGS

Young children often take to computers with great success, even faster than some adults. Kids still in diapers suck their thumbs with one hand, while working a program with the other. What is the best age for children to start? Studies show that when youngsters are given free access to computers, 3-year-olds prefer playing with blocks or sand, 4-year-olds use the computer moderately, and 5-year-olds are enthusiastic.[5] Child development experts say this is because computers are most appropriate for children who are ready to make the transition from concrete to abstract thinking. For many children this change comes toward the end of the preschool period, but this may vary depending on individual differences.[6]

TO BUY OR NOT TO BUY

Advertisements imply that a child is doomed to failure without a computer, that kids must become computer literate as early as possible, and that parents must rush out and buy one immediately. No wonder adults worry that their computerless youngsters will be at an educational disadvantage. This has not been proven, and experts advise against investing in one solely for the preschooler. Educators feel that, at this stage, computers are nice but not necessary. However, if parents are planning to buy one anyway for family use, or if one is already in the home, there is no reason why the youngster should not use it too.

HOW TO JUDGE

The good news is that educational software is getting better; the bad news is that finding it is getting harder. Discount, department, and even some grocery stores are selling software, but prices are still too high to warrant indiscriminate shopping.[7] The following guidelines highlight what to look for in quality software for preschool-age children:

- *Enjoyment.* Good software should stimulate a child's natural curiosity, provide rewarding experiences, and be fun!
- *Ease of use.* The program should be simple to learn and operate, preferably with picture menus, so that after initial instruction children can work independently without adult supervision.
- *Appropriateness.* The level and content of the program should match the child's abilities and interests, and not require more reading skill, manual dexterity, or faster reflexes than the child possesses.
- *Interaction.* Children should be active participants, and be able to initiate and control, not just react to, what happens on the screen.
- *Childproof.* Software must be able to withstand the "preschool pounding" that keyboards often have to endure.
- *Problem-solving skills.* Testing alternative responses and using logic to reach solutions, *not* repetitive drill and practice, spark creative thinking.
- *Multiple levels of difficulty.* Different age or skill levels within one program allow for greater individualization and continued use as the child grows.
- *Technical quality.* High-quality graphics and color and rapid response time motivate and sustain interest; improved

synthesized sound systems that "talk" are particularly good for prereaders.

SHOPPING TIPS

It's a good idea to become acquainted with the variety of available software before buying. Many libraries now provide computers available for use; some even have software home-loan privileges. Whenever possible, packages should be previewed with children prior to purchase because, unless they like it, it won't get used much. Parents should also be aware of exchange, refund, and warranty policies, in case they're dissatisfied or the software is defective. Moreover, in this rapidly changing field, it's important to double-check the program's specifications (e.g., printer, color monitor, disk size, etc.) for computer compatibility, and to buy sparingly because of ever-new technology and options. If more help or information is needed about a particular product, the publisher can be contacted directly. Most software companies maintain toll-free telephone numbers, provide assistance, answer questions, and furnish catalogs upon request.

THE BEST PROGRAMS

Over the years computer software has become increasingly more sophisticated, innovative, and exciting. The titles that follow represent a guide to the highest-rated, most appropriate programs for preschool-age children (see "References" for sources).

For convenience in locating a product with a particular focus, programs have been grouped into categories of literacy, mathematics, thinking and reasoning, and computers and creativity, although in reality these areas are all interrelated. The suggested retail prices may vary according to store, discounting policy, hardware, or home or school edition.

Literacy

At the preschool level, programs devoted to emerging literacy outnumber all others by at least two to one. Letter recognition is the most popular topic; other areas of emphasis include letter sounds, alphabetical order, language development, word identification, and writing.

Alphabet Blocks (Ages 3–6, 1987, $59.95, Macintosh; Bright Star Technology, 1450 114th Ave., S.E., Bellevue, WA 98004, 800-695-1860)

DESCRIPTION: A talking elf, toy soldier, light bulb, and building blocks delightfully teach letter names, sounds, and sequence.

COMMENTS: Visual clues guide children to the correct answers if needed. Requires little or no adult supervision.

Animal Alphabet and Other Things (Ages 3–6, 1986, $39.95, Apple II; Pelican/Queue, 338 Commerce Drive, Fairfield, CT 06430, 800-232-2224)

DESCRIPTION: Letters are magically transformed into animals at the press of a key—R becomes a rhino on roller skates—as a 26-member menagerie advances alphabet abilities.

COMMENTS: Both upper- and lowercase letters are featured. Teacher's Guide contains activities and masters for follow-up practice.

The Berenstain Bears Learn about Letters (3–6, 1991, $39.95, IBM/Compatibles; Tandy Britannica Software, 345 Fourth St., San Francisco, CA 94107, 800-572-2272)

DESCRIPTION: While kids help Brother and Sister Bear search for lost pages of their alphabet book scattered throughout Bearville, they learn about letters, sounds, and directions.

COMMENTS: These adorable bears are also featured in *Fun with Colors,* an electronic coloring book, and *Learn about Counting,* which teaches basic math concepts.

Charlie Brown's ABC's (3–6, 1984, $29.95, Apple, IBM; American School Publishers, distributed by Queue, 338 Commerce Drive, Fairfield, CT 06430, 800-232-2224)

DESCRIPTION: The Peanuts gang takes aim at the alphabet in humorous, animated fashion. Letters and personalized reward certificates can be printed out.

COMMENTS: *Charlie Brown's 1,2,3's* zeros in on number recognition and counting through 10.

Easy as ABC (3–6, 1984, $39.95, Apple, IBM; $49.95, Macintosh; Springboard/Queue, 338 Commerce Drive, Fairfield, CT 06430, 800-232-2224)

DESCRIPTION: Children will make a beeline for this appealing alphabet program (and the jumping frogs will keep them fascinated) as they match letters, connect the dots, and interact with the animals to master letter recognition and sequence.

COMMENTS: No reading is necessary; can be played without adult guidance. Spirited graphics sustain attention.

First Letter Fun (3–6, 1985, $39.95, Apple; MECC, 6160 Summit Drive North, Minneapolis, MN 55430, 800-685-6322)

DESCRIPTION: A farm, circus, park, and magic show are the backdrops for introducing initial sounds. When an object from a story appears on the screen, children match its beginning sound with one of four letters shown.

COMMENTS: This well-animated program includes all letters except Q and X.

Fun from A to Z (3–6, 1985, $39.95, Apple; MECC, 6160 Summit Drive North, Minneapolis, MN 55430, 800-685-6322)

DESCRIPTION: Children discriminate, match, and sequence letters as they help lost birds find their way home, complete dot pictures, and assist animals in winning races.

COMMENTS: Amusing games and puzzles review both upper- and lowercase letter forms.

Muppet Word Book (3–6, 1986, $65, Apple; Sunburst, 101 Castleton St., Pleasantville, NY 10570-3498, 800-628-8897)

DESCRIPTION: The famous Muppets present letters, sounds, word beginnings and endings, plus a miniword processor for writing and spelling. The software can be used on the Muppet Learning Keys, a colorful keyboard tailored especially for young kids, with large letters in alphabetical order, and easy-to-use directional buttons.

COMMENTS: The Learning Keys comes with *Muppets on Stage,* for letter, number, and color recognition. Teacher's Guides are extensive; graphics are excellent.

The Playroom (3–6, 1989, $49.95, Apple, IBM, Macintosh; Broderbund, P.O. Box 6125, Novato, CA 94948-6125, 800-521-6263)

DESCRIPTION: As children enter this playroom, they're exposed to an environment that enhances creativity, enjoyment, and learning. Any toy they select springs to life with animation and sound as Pepper Mouse prompts letter recognition, counting, time concepts, spelling, keyboarding, art, and logic. A little stuffed Pepper Mouse toy is an added bonus.

COMMENTS: Described as setting a new standard for early childhood software, it has been recommended as the one to choose if only one program is possible.[8]

Stone Soup (4 and up, 1989, $75, Apple, IBM; William K. Bradford, 310 School St., Acton, MA 01720, 800-421-2009)

DESCRIPTION: This time-honored tale is one of the *Explore-a-Classic* series that brings literature to life and integrates technology into the language program. Animated texts appear on the screen; children can move characters and objects around as they wish, even design their own stories, and then save or print the results. Absorbing activities, such as puppetry and treasure hunts, also enrich learning.

COMMENTS: Although both this and D. C. Heath's *Explore-a-Story* are intended primarily for beginning readers and up, preschoolers have also profited from these exceptional programs with adult assistance.

Mathematics

In mathematics, software for preschoolers focuses on basic concepts and beginning computation. Specific areas covered in the following programs include number and shape identification, counting, size relationships, and simple addition.

Counting Critters (3–6, 1985, $39.95, Apple; MECC, 6160 Summit Drive North, Minneapolis, MN 55430, 800-685-6322)

DESCRIPTION: Engaging activities, such as counting animals on a safari, matching numbers in a magic show, and supplying a pet store with the correct number of puppies, concentrate on counting and number concepts through 20.

COMMENTS: Program can be adapted to specific numbers and different ability levels. Graphics are lively; sounds are lifelike.

Math and Me (3–6, 1987, $29.95, Apple, IBM; Davidson, 19840 Pioneer Ave., Torrance, CA 90503, 800-545-7677)

DESCRIPTION: Merry monkeys motivate math skills in 12 activities that focus on shapes, numbers, patterns, and addition through nine. At the completion of the program, children receive a personalized award certificate and a coloring book.

COMMENTS: The talking version ($20 more) provides verbal reinforcement.

Mickey's 1,2,3's: The Big Surprise Party (2–5, 1990, $49.95, IBM/Compatibles; Disney, P.O. Box 290, Buffalo, NY 14207-0290, 800-688-1520)

DESCRIPTION: Disney's favorite mouse plans a party with children's input into his actions and decisions. As Mickey scoots around town visiting the post office, toy factory, and grocery store, young programmers have fun learning about numbers through nine.

COMMENTS: *Mickey's ABC's: A Day at the Fair* aids identification of letters and simple words; *Mickey's Jigsaw Puzzles,* with multiple levels of play using 4 to 64 pieces, challenges thinking skills.

The New Talking Stickybear Shapes (3–6, 1989, $49.95, Apple;

$39.95, IBM (with Echo board or Covox); Weekly Reader/Optimum, 10 Station Place, Norfolk, CT 06058, 800-327-1473)

DESCRIPTION: Endearing Stickybear has children pick, name, and find circles, squares, triangles, rectangles, and diamonds in three games that showcase shape identification.

COMMENTS: Other programs in this visually pleasing Stickybear series familiarize children with letters, numbers, and word opposites. They come with such extras as books, stickers, and posters.

Number Farm (3–6, 1984, $32.95, Apple, Commodore, IBM; DLM, One DLM Park, Allen, TX 75002, 800-527-4727)

DESCRIPTION: A country setting with Old MacDonald and his farmyard friends cultivates counting through nine, and such concepts as "greater than" and "less than."

COMMENTS: Activities are carefully sequenced and developmentally appropriate.

Sesame Street Crayon: Numbers Count (3–5, 1987, $12.95, Apple, Commodore, IBM; $19.95, Amiga; Merit, 13635 Gamma Road, Dallas, TX 75244, 800-238-4277)

DESCRIPTION: The Count and the Sesame Street characters star in a coloring book that centers on numbers from one to ten. Children select from a palette of 16 colors to fill in 30 different pictures and, in this mistake-proof program, pictures can be erased and recolored repeatedly, or printed out with a calendar.

COMMENTS: Kids can color their way through the alphabet (*ABC's, Letters for You*), antonyms (*Opposites Attract*), and country scenes (*Fun on the Farm, This Land Is Your Land*) in this inviting, inexpensive series.

Thinking and Reasoning

The programs in this section seek to strengthen perception, discrimination, classification, sequence, and memory skills.

Muppetville (4–6, 1986, $65, Apple; Sunburst, 101 Castleton Street, Pleasantville, NY 10570-3498, 800-628-8897)

DESCRIPTION: Kermit the Frog takes children on a unicycle ride to such places as Animal's House, Gonzo's Zoo, and the Muppet Factory, where they manipulate shapes, symbols, numbers, and colors, and improve thinking and memory skills.

COMMENTS: This highly rated program operates with a regular keyboard, the Muppet Learning Keys, or a Touch Window. It has several levels of difficulty and comes with a suggestion-filled Teacher's Guide.

Observation and Classification (3–5, 1985, $35.95, Apple; Hartley, 133 Bridge St., Dimondale, MI 48821, 800-247-1380)

DESCRIPTION: Four games, in which children note similarities and differences, sharpen skills of sorting familiar objects by use and function. Children can choose from one of three difficulty levels.

COMMENTS: *Colors and Shapes, Patterns and Sequences,* and *Size and Logic,* also in this *Early Discoveries* series, promote problem-solving and thinking skills.

Ollie and Seymour (2–5, 1987, $49.95, Apple; Hartley, 133 Bridge St., Dimondale, MI 48821, 800-247-1380)

DESCRIPTION: As children help Ollie, the balloon man, find Seymour, the monkey, they exercise directionality, thinking, and traffic-safety skills. Other activities in this simulated park and neighborhood accent shape and color recognition, visual memory, and number concepts.

COMMENTS: Guide contains follow-up ideas and reproducible materials.

Computers and Creativity

The following programs provide opportunities for computer familiarity and creativity:

Facemaker, Golden Edition (3–6, 1986, $39.95, Apple, IBM; $44.95, IBM (3.5")); Spinnaker/Qucuc, 338 Commerce Drive, Fairfield, CT 06430, 800-232-2224)

DESCRIPTION: Children fashion funny faces (from a selection of eyes, ears, noses, etc.), make features move (eyes wink, ears wiggle, mouths smile), and play memory games while rehearsing computer and concentration skills.

COMMENTS: This program has been a long-time best seller (over 100,000 sold).

Katie's Farm (2–5, 1990, $39.95, Amiga, Apple IIGS, IBM, Macintosh; Lawrence, 1800 South 35th St., Galesburg, MI 49053-9687, 800-421-4157)

DESCRIPTION: Youngsters learn about computers and farm life in this imaginative interactive adventure. Katie and cousin McGee gather eggs, pick berries, catch fish, and more in this rural ramble through a barn, chicken coop, garden, and pond. Children control areas and activities they want to investigate by selecting one of four pictures displayed at the bottom of the screen.

COMMENTS: Ease of operation and all-picture format make this a fine first computer experience. Sounds (squeaking buckets, squawking chickens, neighing horses) are realistic; humor predominates.

Kid Pix (3–7, 1991, $59.95 (Dual Pack), IBM, Macintosh; Broderbund, P.O. Box 6125, Novato, CA 94948-6125, 800-521-6263)

DESCRIPTION: This highly original painting program can turn any preschooler into a Picasso. It's loaded with tools and options, such as 28 wacky brushes, 100 picture stamps, a talking alphabet (in English and Spanish), and sensational sound effects. The silly erasers (firecrackers, black holes, fade-aways, and drop-outs) make a mistake almost as much fun as a masterpiece.

COMMENTS: A "Small Kids Mode" protects other applications from youthful accidents. This and another top-rated program for kids 3–10, *Color Me* (Mindscape, 800-829-1900), allow for both open-ended and more structured art experiences.

McGee at the Fun Fair (2–5, 1991, $39.95, Amiga, Apple IIGS; $24.95, IBM, Macintosh; Lawrence, 1800 South 35th St., Galesburg, MI 49053-9687, 800-421-4157)

DESCRIPTION: With a click of the mouse, kids can make McGee and pal Tony swing on the monkey bars, listen to a one-man band, watch a juggler, or choose other carnival capers. This is a sequel to *McGee,* an early morning toddler's household exploration.

COMMENTS: These "No-Words Software" help children become computer comfortable, and also stimulate language development, spatial relationships, and eye–hand coordination.

Slight variations in responses are programmed to maintain novelty.

FREE OR INEXPENSIVE MATERIALS

Apple Computer, Inc., 20330 Stevens Creek Boulevard, M/S 36-AN, Cupertino, CA 95014.

Macintosh Educational Software Guide, Jeffrey H. Orloff, ed. A comprehensive, informative guide to highly rated educational software packages for the Macintosh computer that covers many subject areas. Of particular interest are the 48 entries in the "Early Learning" section. A free copy is available by sending a written request to Customer Relations at the above address.

Southern Early Childhood Association, Box 5403, Brady Station, Little Rock, AR 72215, 501-663-0353.

Appropriate Uses of Computers in the Early Childhood Curriculum, Kevin J. Swick. This position statement covers such topics as the role, place, and appropriate uses of computers with young children, and the involvement of children and staff. 40¢.

Chapter 5

Magazines

"They sure don't make kids' magazines like they used to," declared *US News & World Report.*[1] The new breed is stylish and sophisticated; the photography and illustrations are top drawer, the writing lively, and the design sleek and inviting.[2] And with the increased interest in preschool and child care programs, more and more publishers are now providing "under 5" magazines.[3]

Preschool magazines have also become increasingly diverse, spanning a range of topics and interests. Some focus on specific themes: *Your Big Backyard* highlights nature and conservation; *Chickadee* stresses the environment; *Turtle* and *Humpty Dumpty's Magazine* are health-oriented; *Happy Times* seeks to foster religious and moral values. Popular television and cartoon characters are featured in *Sesame Street* and *Mickey Mouse; Funday, Let's Find Out, My First Magazine,* and *Surprise* are school weeklies. Of course, the granddaddy of them all, *Highlights for Children,* which bridges many subject areas, is still going strong.

WHY YOUNG CHILDREN LIKE MAGAZINES[4]

- Magazines grab and hold attention. Their colorful covers motivate youngsters to look inside, and their bold, visually exciting illustrations keep their interest.
- Magazines are entertaining. Their professional style and content are especially designed to delight and stimulate young minds.
- Magazine features are short. Preschoolers enjoy the satisfaction of being able to complete a story or activity in a brief period of time.
- Magazines offer variety. A single issue usually contains a mix of stories, pictures, activities, puzzles, as well as different styles of writing.
- Children love to receive mail, and they take special pleasure in the regular arrival of magazines addressed to them personally.
- Magazines are lightweight and portable. They can be carried, rolled, bent, or stuffed into a pocket, pocketbook, or bookbag.

WHY PARENTS/CAREGIVERS LIKE THEM TOO[5]

- Magazines are an enriching supplement to books, and may open up new avenues of reading pleasure.
- Magazines focus on children's special interests, and help to develop new ones.
- Magazines are inexpensive. A full year's subscription usually costs less than one hardcover book.
- Magazine subscriptions make great gifts, and keep kids reading all year long.

- Magazines offer children a chance to get involved by inviting them to submit original artwork, jokes, stories, or questions for publication.
- And, it bears repeating, magazines make learning fun!

Bernice Cullinan, an authority on children's literature and a past president of the International Reading Association, sums it up well: "Children's magazines are a bridge to literacy. Many of them contain high-quality writing, entertaining activities, and topical information. When they are available in the home, the school, and the library, they entice readers to sample their contents, and support the reading habit."[6]

TIPS FOR CHOOSING AND USING

When choosing a magazine, it is important to consider a child's age, interests, and abilities. It is also a good idea to preview a copy, to make sure it is suitable and the youngster likes it, before investing money in a subscription. The most popular magazines, with the highest circulations, can usually be found at newsstands or bookstores. Schools or libraries have a broader selection and are good sources of back issues. Most periodicals, however, are available only through subscription, but publishers will usually furnish a sample upon request. New subscribers should also check to see whether special introductory rates are available.

Preschoolers generally enjoy their magazines more when reading them with an adult. Parents and caregivers can enrich this sharing and learning experience by showing the pictures, reading the words or stories, and assisting with the activities.[7] Suggestions for using each issue with follow-up ideas are typically included.

Publishers are concerned about their audience and are sensitive to feedback. Readers can have a powerful impact and effect changes by writing to the publisher about what they like, don't like, or would like in the magazine.

OLD MAGAZINES NEVER DIE: SUGGESTIONS FOR FOLLOW-UP USE

Magazines have many useful lives. Children enjoy rereading old issues the way they do favorite books. They like to return to their favorite parts, hear a touching story, look at a startling photograph, or laugh at a humorous antic again and again. Reading Is Fundamental, a national organization that works to improve literacy, advises, "After you've read them, don't throw your magazines away!" They recommend the following ways in which old magazines can be recycled for fun and learning.[8]

- *Cut-and-paste pictures.* The preschooler can find and cut out pictures and paste on pages labeled with letters, colors, shapes, and other early concepts.
- *Shopping lists.* Young shoppers can cut and paste pictures to make up their own lists, or a wish list for Santa or birthdays.
- *Story starters.* A young storyteller can talk or write about what is happening in an interesting photo.
- *Telegrams.* Beginning readers can cut out words they recognize and assemble them in short messages to make telegrams.
- *Rebus stories.* Children can make up colorful sentences and stories, substituting picture cutouts for some of the words or sounds.
- *Posters.* Full-page photos and artwork from a magazine can be tacked up as posters.

- *Jigsaw puzzles.* A full-page picture from a magazine can be pasted on a piece of cardboard and then cut up for a jigsaw puzzle.

A GUIDE TO THE BEST

The following section provides information on the most current magazines available for preschool-age children. Each entry contains the title, targeted age level, price, number of issues per year, policy regarding samples, design format, publisher, description, and comments. The ones preceded by a star are particularly recommended.

Home Subscriptions

★*Chickadee* (Ages 3–9, $14.95, 10 issues, 32 pp., 8¼″ × 10¾″, Sample, $3.75; Young Naturalist Foundation, 255 Great Arrow Avenue, Buffalo, NY 14207-3082, 416-868-6001)

DESCRIPTION: Superb wildlife photographs and pictures highlight this Canadian publication designed to interest children in the environment and the world around them. It is also filled with stories, poems, projects, experiments, puzzles, observation games, and such thought-provoking features as "Did You Know" and "What Is It." Letters and pictures from readers and a centerfold poster are other regular attractions.

COMMENTS: Like *Owl*—for kids over eight from the same publisher—this magazine is both challenging and stimulating. Eye-catching illustrations are outstanding. Preschoolers will need adult guidance.

Happy Times (Ages 3–5, $6.95, 12 issues, 16 pp., 8″ × 8¼″, Sample, free; Concordia Publishing House, 3558 South Jefferson Ave., St. Louis, MO 63118-3975, 314-268-1000, Fax: 314-268-1329)

DESCRIPTION: This Lutheran monthly seeks to strengthen and support Christian home training through stories, poems, songs, games, puzzles, and other activities that stress the teaching of God and moral values. A "Grown-Ups' page," included in most issues, acts as a guide. The magazine is meant to be read together by parent and child to promote interaction and closeness.

COMMENTS: Circulation is through individual subscription, in bulk for preschool and Sunday School classes, and also on a quarterly basis for Sunday School customers. Bulk rates to the same address are discounted.

Highlights for Children (2–12, $21.67, 11 issues, 44 pp., 8⅜" × 10⅞", Sample, free; Highlights for Children, P.O. Box 182167, Columbus, OH 43218-2167, 800-255-9517)

DESCRIPTION: The "fun with a purpose" concept of this long-time favorite is aimed at developing basic skills, thinking and reasoning, creativity, and high ideals. The diverse menu includes stories, poems, games, puzzles, riddles, crafts, projects, holiday features, and other activities. Children are encouraged to send in original drawings, poems, and stories. A guide for parents and teachers indicates the skill emphasis of each article.

COMMENTS: The great variety of subjects on many levels is good when the magazine is shared by children of different ages, but preschoolers will need adult assistance. Stories and features have a wholesome, moral tone.

Humpty Dumpty's Magazine (4–6, $13.95, 8 issues, 48 pp., 6⅛"

× 9⅛," Sample, 75¢; Children's Better Health Institute, Humpty Dumpty's Magazine, P.O. Box 10902, Des Moines, IA 50306, 800-444-2704)

DESCRIPTION: The accent is on nutrition, exercise, hygiene, and safety with stories, poems, hidden pictures, connect-the-dots, mazes, puzzles, crafts, and seasonal and holiday activities. Regular features include "Humpty at Home," a two-page cartoon, simple healthy recipes, and original artwork. A page for parents and teachers answers health-related questions.

COMMENTS: The other five periodicals from this publisher committed to health education for children are *Turtle,* ages 2–5; *Children's Playmate,* ages 6–8; *Jack and Jill,* ages 7–10; *Child's Life,* ages 9–11; *Children's Digest,* preteen. Youngsters will need help reading this magazine.

★*Ladybug* (2–7, $29.97, 12 issues, 36 pp., 8″ × 9¼," Sample, send $2.00 to Ladybug Sample Issue, P.O. Box 300, Peru, IL 61354; Ladybug, P.O. Box 58342, Boulder, CO 80322-8342, 800-888-6995)

DESCRIPTION: This beautifully produced, full-color monthly for toddlers, preschoolers, and beginning readers inspires a love of reading and learning. It features prominent early childhood authors and artists, fine stories, poems, songs, rhymes, games, and activity pages with projects to cut, match, color, and draw. There is also a six-page insert with information and suggestions for parents.

COMMENTS: The quality art and literature continues the high standards set by *Cricket,* the acclaimed literary magazine for children aged 6–12 from the same publisher.

Mickey Mouse (2–6, $10.30, 4 issues plus an annual, 40 pp., 8″ × 10⅞," Sample, free; Mickey Mouse Magazine, P.O. Box 10598, Des Moines, IA 50340, 515-247-7500)

DESCRIPTION: The famous Disney characters merrily present opportunities for fun and learning with stories, articles, rhymes, connect-the-dots, coloring, and other activities. "Mickey's Mail" and "Goofy's Giggles" showcase letters, jokes, and riddles from readers. The second part of the magazine is a "Guide for Grown-ups," with ideas for family sharing, recipes, and crafts.

COMMENTS: The presentation is professional and engaging; the parent's section informative and entertaining. Some advertisements are included.

★*Sesame Street* (2–6, $14.97, 10 issues, 34 pp., 8⅛″ × 10¾″, Sample, free; Sesame Street Magazine, P.O. Box 55518, Boulder, CO 80322-2000, 800-678-0613)

DESCRIPTION: For more than 20 years, this publication has made learning an adventure, with richly instructive, imaginatively creative offerings. Just as on the popular television show, Ernie, Bert, and their Muppet friends deftly explore basic concepts, positive social skills, and preschool feelings with stories, poems, games, puzzles, and more. Children are invited to contribute drawings, poems, and letters. A separate, extensive "Parents' Guide" contains articles on child development and tips for enhancing the children's magazine.

COMMENTS: The lively, activity-filled format is engrossing, the vibrant illustrations entice, and the "Parents' Guide" is exceptional.

Turtle Magazine for Preschool Kids (2–5, $13.95, 8 issues, 48 pp., 6⅛″ × 9⅛″, Sample, 75¢; Children's Better Health Institute, Turtle Magazine, P.O. Box 10902, Des Moines, IA 50306, 800-444-2704)

DESCRIPTION: Like the other five titles from this publisher, this periodical stresses healthy living. It includes stories, poems, rebus rhymes, puzzles, hidden pictures, connect-the-dots, and other readiness activities. Regular features include "Our Own Pictures," drawn by the readers, and a page for parents and teachers that addresses health concerns.

COMMENTS: Although the magazine teaches fundamentals of nutrition, exercise, and safety in simple terms, youngsters will need help to fully appreciate the message. Provides opportunities for reader involvement.

★*Your Big Backyard* (3–5, $12, 12 issues, 20 pp., 8″ × 10″, Sample not available; National Wildlife Federation, 1400 Sixteenth St., N.W., Washington, DC 20036, 800-432-6564)

DESCRIPTION: The world and wonders of nature are captured in this highly pictorial monthly through stunning wildlife photography, read-to-me stories, poems, puzzles, games, and crafts. A parent's letter offers follow-up learning recommendations.

COMMENTS: This preschool version of *Ranger Rick* is on a three-year repeating cycle; after 36 issues it returns to the first. The spectacular close-up photographs and easy captions spur an interest in reading and conservation.

School Magazines and Newspapers

The following magazines are primarily intended for group distribution, such as school or day-care settings. Individual home subscriptions are also available at approximately twice the bulk rate, which is still very reasonable.

★*Let's Find Out* (Ages 5, $4.95 (10 or more subscriptions), 32 issues, 4 pp., 8″ × 10⅞″, Sample, free; Scholastic, P.O. Box 3710, Jefferson City, MO 65102-9957, 800-631-1586)

DESCRIPTION: Kindergarten kids build early learning skills and expand their world with this activity-based newspaper. Organized around a central theme, it covers holidays, seasons, and other events with "read-to-me" stories, classroom calendars, games, activities, and take-home material. Each of the eight monthly packages includes four 2-page magazines, a teacher's guide, posters, learning games, task cards, and parents' newsletters written in English and Spanish.

COMMENTS: Visually pleasing, it motivates questioning and curiosity. Small-print text is meant to be read to children.

★*My First Magazine* (Ages 3–4, $3.75 (10 or more subscriptions), 24 issues, 4 pp., 7¾″ × 9″, Sample, free; Scholastic, P.O. Box 3710, Jefferson City, MO 65102-9957, 800-631-1586)

DESCRIPTION: The publishers of *Pre-K Today* offer early learning experiences with an emphasis on social–emotional growth, literacy, and family ties within a delightful, developmentally appropriate context. Each of the six thematic monthly packs contains four issues, with its own separate focus, foldout posters, teacher's guides, and monthly "Parent Pages," with insights and tips, in both Spanish and English.

COMMENTS: Well-suited to the interests and needs of young children. Extension suggestions and advice are useful for both parent and teacher.

Weekly Reader Funday (Ages 3–4, $3.90 (5 or more subscriptions), 24 issues, 4 pp., 8⅛″ × 11⅜″, Sample, free to teachers; Newfield Publications, 4343 Equity Drive, Columbus, OH 43216, 800-999-7100)

DESCRIPTION: Banana Monkey and his frisky friends, along with picture stories, puzzles, and games, teach language, thinking, science, and social skills. Suggestions for teacher or parent at the bottom of the page act as a guide. Each monthly package contains four issues, one of which is a minibook, a curriculum unit with reproducible "Parent Notes" in English and Spanish, and a poster-sized supplement.

COMMENTS: This pre-kindergarten picture weekly is the first of a well-known series of classroom newspapers that extends through grade six. Teaching tips are helpful; photographs and drawings are large and colorful.

Weekly Reader Surprise (Age 5, $2.50 (10 or more subscriptions), 24 issues, 4 pp., 8⅛" × 11⅜", Sample, free to teachers; Newfield Publications, 4343 Equity Drive, Columbus, OH 43216, 800-999-7100)

DESCRIPTION: The amusing antics of Zip the dog, Nip the cat, and their animal friends, combined with pictures, photos, and simple vocabulary, strengthen literacy, social, and science skills in this kindergarten weekly. Directions and tips for teachers and parents are at the bottom of each page. A teacher's edition is also included to help use the paper effectively.

COMMENTS: Material is nicely paced and age-appropriate. The artwork is abundant and appealing.

Chapter 6

Toys and Games

Toys are terrific! Everyone loves them—kids and adults alike. What makes it even better is that toys are actually good for preschoolers. While they are having fun, children are learning about the world, and their place in it, and they are growing physically, mentally, emotionally, and socially. Tricycles and balls, for example, help develop gross motor skills; puzzles promote problem solving and finger dexterity. Creativity is spurred with crayons and clay; imagination and role playing flourish when children play with dolls. Matching games help improve memory and concentration, while group play teaches about sharing and getting along with others. And the list goes on. Since play is so vital to development, it is often called "child's work," and toys, "the tools for learning."

HOW TO CHOOSE

With the thousands of toys on the market and the constant bombardment of advertising hype, it's often difficult, if not nearly impossible, to know how to select good toys. And with the high price of high tech, making a mistake can be costly. The following considerations will help parents and caregivers to make wise choices.

Toys should be:

- *Safe.* They must be strong and durable enough to withstand all kinds of kid use and abuse. They should have no exposed pins, wires, nails, or sharp edges, and they should be made with nontoxic, lead-free material. And, most importantly, they must contain no small parts that present choking hazards (see Appendix for U.S. Consumer Product Safety Commission regulations).
- *Appropriate to age and abilities.* Toys should not be too easy or too hard, providing both satisfaction and challenge. A good rule of thumb is to select those that are just slightly above the child's present level; anything more advanced will be too frustrating.
- *Appealing and interesting.* Toys that match individual tastes and preferences have better "repeat-play value." Parents, who know their kids better than anyone else, should trust their own judgment about which toys their youngsters would probably like.
- *Varied.* A balance of different types of toys expands learning. A good mix covers a wide range of experiences and provides for large body movement, hands-on activities, dramatic play, experimentation, and inspiration.
- *Able to be used in many ways.* Blocks, for example, can become a tower, a train, or a tightrope. Diverse uses for such flexible, "open-ended" toys stimulate creative thinking and extend the life of the toy.

PLAYTHINGS FOR CHILDREN WITH SPECIAL NEEDS

Children with physical or learning handicaps, as well as those who are intellectually gifted, often require special care and consideration in the selection of toys. These children have the same desire for play as any other child, and appropriate toys can provide pleasure, build important skills, and bolster self-esteem. A clear picture of the child's strengths and limitations helps in determining what is suitable, and the child's teacher, therapist, or doctor can often provide excellent advice. Many mainstream toys can be used with little or no modifications, but specialized items are available only from certain companies. These are indicated by the symbol (S) in the toy catalog section; the chapter on professional organizations contains additional resources ready to help.

THE BEST PRESCHOOL PLAYTHINGS

Perfect preschool playthings are fun, safe, constructive, and affordable. The following top toys and great games all fit these criteria, and have been recommended by knowledgeable experts in the field (see "References"). They concentrate on the cherished classics of childhood but also include some of the niftiest newer products.

Toys have been grouped into four main types—active, manipulative, make-believe, and creative—which contribute to growth and development in different areas. Of course, many toys fit into more than one category. Riding a small car, for example, provides practice in both active and make-believe play.

Some manufacturers do not sell directly to the public, but their addresses and telephone numbers are furnished in case more information is desired. Prices are included as a general guide, but they vary according to location, store, and discounting policy.

This is a good place to remind parents that toys need not be store-bought. Many common household items—such as boxes, cooking utensils, and clothing—are free, readily available, and just as entertaining and educational as many commercially made products. The age-old "wooden spoon and pot" combo is still hard to beat.

Active Play

Preschoolers are brimming over with boundless energy. They love to run, gallop, climb, and engage in all sorts of active, physical play. They like to take risks, test their skill (jumping from heights, hanging by arms), and perform acrobatics (turning somersaults). They can throw and retrieve all kinds of objects, and ride three- and four-wheel pedal toys with agility. By age five, gross motor skills are well developed, and children are ready for full-sized wagons, scooters, small bicycles, and ball games with simple rules and scoring.

Toys in this category provide opportunities to exercise large muscles and improve strength and coordination. Examples of this type include push-and-pull toys (doll carriages, small wheelbarrows, and adultlike vacuums and lawn mowers), ride-on vehicles (rocking horses, tricycles, cars), and sports and gym equipment (balls, skates, slides, swings).

Airplane Teeter Totter (2–6, $55–75; Little Tikes, 2180 Barlow Road, Hudson, OH 44236, 800-321-0183)

DESCRIPTION: A new twist on the old see-saw. Add a propeller and tail, and presto—it's also a plane that can spin around 360°. Pilots can fly solo or take on two passengers. The wide circular base prevents crash landings.

COMMENTS: Children aged 4 and older will probably enjoy this one more than 2- and 3-year-olds.

Garden Tractor (3–6, $40–55; Little Tikes, 2180 Barlow Road, Hudson, OH 44236, 800-321-0183)

DESCRIPTION: Is that the gardener steering this sturdy tricycle-tractor, or just the preschooler pretending? A companion *Garden Cart,* sold separately, is a great add-on.

COMMENTS: *Toddler Tractor and Cart* are available for tykes 1½ to 3.

Magic Vac (2–6, $15–20; Fisher-Price, 636 Gerard Ave., East Aurora, NY 14052, 800-432-5437)

DESCRIPTION: Housework is child's play with this kid-version carpet cleaner. It lights up and makes noise when it is pushed, and has a handle that folds flat to fit under furniture. This machine looks and sounds real. The only complaint parents may have is that it isn't! Comes fully assembled; no batteries required.

COMMENTS: 2- and 3-year-olds particularly like household and cooking equipment (stove, refrigerator) and adultlike push toys (lawnmower, shopping cart) for domestic imitation and role playing.

1-2-3 Roller Skates (3–6, $16; Fisher-Price, 636 Gerard Ave., East Aurora, NY 14052, 800-432-5437)

DESCRIPTION: Learning to skate can be scary, but these skates make it easier. The three-setting process takes beginners from just walking, to getting the "feel" of the wheels, to forward motion only—with no danger of rolling in reverse—to the final "freewheeling" stage. Either-foot skates, and Velcro fasteners (no buckles or laces), are other child-friendly features. Can be adjusted to fit shoe sizes 6–12.

COMMENTS: Balancing on skates is more geared to older pre-schoolers (4 and 5). Wheels should be made of plastic and have no ball bearings for reduced speed.

Super Car (1½–5, $60–70; Today's Kids, P.O. Box 207, Booneville, AR 72927, 800-258-TOYS)

DESCRIPTION: Beep, beep! Here comes the little cruiser in a convertible. Loaded with options, it comes complete with push-back top and sunroof, working ignition key and horn, swiveling sideview mirror, clicking gears, and behind-the-seat storage. As motorists drive this foot-propelled minimobile, they gain mastery of motor skills as well as a feeling of being "in control."

COMMENTS: This toy comes with a three-year guarantee that is standard for the company. *Cozy Coupe* (Little Tikes) is an additional auto alternative.

Super Trike (2–5, $35–45; Today's Kids, P.O. Box 207, Booneville, AR 72927, 800-258-TOYS)

DESCRIPTION: Little pedal pushers practice coordination and balance as they cycle around on this ride-on toy. It features large wheels for stability, front-tread wheel for traction, durable plastic construction, and an adjustable seat.

COMMENTS: Also recommended are Preskools's *1,2,3 First Bike,* which takes beginners from foot pushing to two-wheel riding by adjusting or removing the training wheels, and Fisher-Price's *Tough Trike.*

Toddler Basketball (9–36 months, $20; Playskool, P.O. Box 200, Pawtucket, RI 02862-0200, 800-PLAYSKL)

DESCRIPTION: Even the littlest hoopster can score big with the easy-to-grasp ball, bell that rings with every shot, and squeaker button that activates a pop-up surprise. Tots can graduate to Little Tike's *Basketball Set* with an adjustable 4', 5', or 6' backboard.

COMMENTS: Preschoolers are partial to ball playing. By age 4, amateur athletes can "batter up" with a soft, lightweight baseball, and begin playing with junior-sized soccer and footballs.

Manipulative Play

Preschoolers have their hands on and in everything. They love to put things together (and then take them apart again). They are busy buttoning, building, mixing, and matching. Increasing finger control lets them pick up small objects, cut on a line with scissors, grasp a pencil, and string beads.

Manipulative playthings develop fine motor skills, hand–eye coordination, conceptualization, and creativity. Types of toys that fit this category include blocks, construction sets, puzzles, pegboards, lacing and stringing toys, and sorting games.

Blocks (2 and up, Sets, $37–120; Childcraft, P.O. Box 29149, Mission, KS 66201-9149, 800-631-5657)

DESCRIPTION: One of the most valued and valuable of toys, blocks provide countless open-ended opportunities for constructing and creating. Their many benefits include stimulation of imagination, symbolic thought, spatial relationships, and motor skills. Childcraft's quality wooden blocks come in variably priced sets, but individual units (curves, arches, columns, etc.) can also be purchased separately.

COMMENTS: Serviceable blocks can also be made of strong cardboard (*Super Bricks,* Toys to Grow On) and plastic (*Mega*

Blocks, Retvik). Accessories, such as people, vehicles, animals, and signs, add to the experience.

Candyland (3–6, $7; Milton Bradley, 443 Shaker Road, East Longmeadow, MA 01028-5247, 413-525-6411)

DESCRIPTION: The candy cane letters in the game's title will bring back fond memories to parents who played it themselves as children. Now it is their offspring's turn to move the gingerbread men to the castle at the end of the path. Along the way, they will learn about matching and playing with others. For two to four players.

COMMENTS: Preschoolers hate to lose and are generally not ready for competitive play. First board games must be based completely on chance, not strategy, have few rules, and no reading beyond ABC.

Capital Magnetic Letters (3–6, $4.49; Playskool, P.O. Box 200, Pawtucket, RI 02862-0200, 800-PLAYSKL)

DESCRIPTION: Whether used for identifying letters, forming words, or putting in ABC order, these letters lead to literacy. *Magnetic Numbers* and the *Magnetic Spelling Board* are perfect partners for the alphabet.

COMMENTS: Parents need to be concerned about toy size. Young children, especially those under 3, are likely to put objects in their mouths, so parts must be too large to swallow (more than 1½″ in diameter).

DUPLO Basic Building Sets (1½–5, $7–$50; LEGO, Enfield, CT 06083-1138, 800-422-5346)

DESCRIPTION: Big, bright, lightweight blocks and shapes fit together to lay the foundation for building fun. Theme sets

(*Children's Zoo, Gas Station, Fire Dispatch,* etc.) and specialty pieces (clown, lion) are show extenders. LEGO, colorful bricks and figures that interlock with DUPLO, are for kids 3–12.

COMMENTS: Individual models can be added at any time, making great gift ideas. LEGO sets contain small parts not suitable for children under 3 years of age; care must be taken to keep them out of reach of younger siblings.

The Original Memory (3–6, $7; Milton Bradley, 443 Shaker Road, East Longmeadow, MA 01028-5247, 413-525-6411)

DESCRIPTION: Can you remember what's hiding where? That's the challenge facing children as they try to find pairs of picture cards in this Concentration-like game. Others in the series are *Animal Families,* uniting baby animals with their parents, and *Mickey Mouse,* pairing Disney characters. Each can be played solo or in groups; no reading is required.

COMMENTS: Focusing attention and noting similarities help children in the reading process.

Original Rollercoaster (1½–5, $15–25; Anatex, 15929 Arminta St., Van Nuys, CA 91406, 800-999-9599)

DESCRIPTION: Bright beads slide up, down, and around to captivate children, and motivate manipulation and tracking skills.

COMMENTS: Chunky, connecting cranks and gears also coordinate hand and eye in *Busy Gears* by Playskool.

Puzzles (2 and up, generic, various manufacturers and prices)

DESCRIPTION: Puzzles charm and challenge as they promote manual dexterity and problem-solving abilities. Ones with knobs firmly attached (4–12 pieces) are preferable for 2-year-olds. Fit-in, framed (20–50 pieces), and jigsaw puzzles (10–25 pieces) will please 3- to 5-year-olds.

COMMENTS: Dressing, stringing, and nesting toys, color forms, lock boxes, and pegboards also foster fine motor control.

See 'N Say (1½–5, $10; Mattel, 333 Continental Blvd., El Segundo, CA 90245-5012, 800-421-2887)

DESCRIPTION: Point and pull is the basic principle in these picture–sound association games. Now activated by a lever instead of a string, preschoolers seem as fascinated as ever watching them spin and hearing them "talk." Separate models focus on animals, colors, counting, letters, and nursery rhymes.

COMMENTS: Involving several senses at the same time (seeing, hearing, talking, feeling, and sometimes even tasting) reinforces the message and aids learning.

Tinkertoys (3½ and up, $7–$17; Playskool, P.O. Box 200, Pawtucket, RI 02862-0200, 800-PLAYSKL)

DESCRIPTION: Spools, rods, wheels, swirls, and connectors are some components of this classic construction set. Kids can build their own free-form structures or erect more realistic, representational ones.

COMMENTS: Remember that small parts are a choking hazard. *Lincoln Logs* (Playskool), another put-together perennial, is for children aged 4–10.

Touch and Tell (2–5, $35–$50; Texas Instruments, P.O. Box 53, Lubbock, TX 79408, 800-TI-CARES)

DESCRIPTION: Cows go "moo," cars go "beep beep," as children put their hands on the touch-sensitive picture panel. Awareness of objects, shapes, and words is encouraged; expansion packs cover letters, numbers, animals, etc. In *Touch and Discover,* Disney pals are the guide to the alphabet, numbers, and more; *My Little Computer* concentrates on computer familiarity.

COMMENTS: Electronic toys have also been used successfully with special-needs children. Despite all their pizzazz, some educators feel that the right–wrong format of many high-tech toys limits divergent thinking.

Make-Believe Play

All the world's a stage for the preschooler. Masters of make-believe, young children love to dress up and "be" Mommy and Daddy. This period of intense interest in dramatic play, with all sorts of costumes and props, peaks at the age of 5. Kids like to pretend by themselves, with their favorite toys and teddies, with other children, and maybe even with an imaginary friend.

Pretend play affords children a chance to engage in fantasy, fuel imagination, express feelings, and "try out" various roles. Dolls, stuffed animals, puppets, play scenes, and toy cars and trains are all included in this grouping.

Busy Dressy Bessy (1–5, $12.99; Playskool, P.O. Box 200, Pawtucket, RI 02862-0200, 800-PLAYSKL)

DESCRIPTION: An updated version of the famous original, this is still the same huggable, "learn-to-dress" doll. Five activities keep youngsters zipping, tying, buckling, buttoning, and snapping as they acquire basic dressing skills. *Dress-Me-Up*

Ernie is the companion practice doll for boys. Both are machine washable and dryable.

COMMENTS: Two-year-olds like soft-bodied and rubber baby dolls as well as realistic ones that fit in their arms. As youngsters grow, they want dolls with more details and features. Five-year-olds are drawn to child-proportioned dolls. In general, the simpler the doll, the more freedom it allows for imaginative play.

Cabbage Patch Dolls/Kids (3 and up, $18–$45; Hasbro, P.O. Box 200, Pawtucket, RI 02862-0200, 800-PLAYSKL)

DESCRIPTION: These puffy, pudgy dolls come with individual birth certificates, names, expressions, and personalities. They created a sensation when they were first introduced and continue to appeal. Be prepared to adopt one into your home.

COMMENTS: Dolls are the most treasured and universal of toys. They provide outlets for emotions, opportunities for reenacting roles, and objects to love and befriend.

Medical Kit (3–7, $16; Fisher-Price, 636 Gerard Ave., East Aurora, NY 14052, 800-432-5437)

DESCRIPTION: Open wide! The doctor is making house calls with this black bag filled with nine props for fantasy play. Includes a working stethoscope, blood pressure gauge, thermometer, reflex hammer, eye chart, and other "tools of the trade."

COMMENTS: Ideal for recreating adult occupations (a favorite pastime of preschoolers), or for preparing for visits to the doctor.

Mickey's Call Back Phone (2 and up, $29; Mattel, 333 Continental Blvd., El Segundo, CA 90245-5012, 800-421-2887)

DESCRIPTION: On this phone youngsters can dial and hear one of the Disney gang. After they hang up, the phone rings, and it's Mickey, Goofy, or Minnie with a return call. Children can hear their own conversation on *The Record and Play Back Telephone* (Fisher-Price). Whatever the extras, and none are needed, the telephone is a true communication classic.

COMMENTS: Parents should rehearse with their children how to call 911 in an emergency and give their address to the operator.

Mighty Tonka Dump (3 and up, $12; Tonka/Hasbro, P.O. Box 200, Pawtucket, RI 02862-0200, 800-PLAYSKL)

DESCRIPTION: For 50 years, this rugged, tilt-back dumper has delighted truckers of all ages. Its versatility adds to its value; it can carry all kinds of cargo (sand, soil, blocks, etc.), be used indoors and out, and alone or with other toys.

COMMENTS: For kids 1½–5: Tonka *Preschool Trucks* come equipped with play people and self-contained storage.

My Buddy (1 and up, $20–$25; Playskool, P.O. Box 200, Pawtucket, RI 02862-0200, 800-PLAYSKL)

DESCRIPTION: Dressed in overalls, cap, and sneakers, this boy doll is always ready for play or hugs. Parents will welcome that he is machine washable, and can be dressed in infant clothing sized 3 to 6 months.

COMMENTS: Boys, as well as girls, like to play with dolls, and enjoy the closeness and security a special plaything can provide.

Play Kitchen (2–6, $65–$90; Little Tikes, 2180 Barlow Road, Hudson, OH 44236, 800-321-0183)

DESCRIPTION: Fledgling chefs can cook, cater, clean up (and copy their adult counterparts) to their heart's content. This all-in-one unit contains sink, range, oven, folding table, coffee maker, cordless play phone, and chalkboard.

COMMENTS: Play scenes, such as home, garage, farm, airport, firehouse, are also dynamite for dramatization, but minimodel inhabitants can present choking threats.

Plush Animal Puppets (3 and up, $5.95 each, $34.80 for six; Constructive Playthings, 1227 East 119th St., Grandview, MO 64030-1117, 800-255-6124)

DESCRIPTION: Youthful puppeteers can perform, pantomime, put on a play, project their feelings, and practice language skills with any of these six animal puppets (rabbit, rooster, duck, dog, lion, elephant) with big, easy-to-manipulate mouths.

COMMENTS: Hand and soft puppets that double as stuffed toys are advisable for 2-year-olds; 3- and 4-year-olds also like sock, mitten, and finger puppets. Hand-and-arm puppets are appreciated at age 5. Making simple puppets with sticks, bags, or socks can be an inexpensive, enjoyable, shared experience.

Wooden Railway (3–10, Sets—$20–$200; BRIO Scanditoy, 6555 W. Mill Road, Milwaukee, WI 53218-1240, 800-558-6863)

DESCRIPTION: Ah, the magic and memory of trains! This wonderful wooden system can grow with the child, by adding on track and accessories (tunnels, bridges, vehicles), into an elaborate playscape. The interchangeable pieces, connecting simply and safely with magnets, allow them to be combined and recombined to keep young engineers and conductors riding the rails for hours.

COMMENTS: This open-ended toy kindles imagination and increases understanding of size and space concepts. Good for independent or cooperative play. Lifelike cars and trucks with moving parts are other top transportation toys.

Creative Play

Painting, pasting, and working with putty are popular preschool pastimes. When left to their own devices, and a little adult support, young artists seem perfectly content to experiment and explore, and they are not overly concerned, until about 4, with the final product. Just as well, for creations often bear little resemblance to reality. Two- to five-year-olds also enjoy making music and responding to it in their own unique ways.

Arts and crafts materials, musical instruments, and audiovisual equipment—channels for creativity play—all help to foster self-expression, concept development, and appreciation of beauty.

Crayons (2–8, $2.50–$4.50; Crayola/Binney & Smith, 1100 Church Lane, P.O. Box 431, Easton, PA 18044-0431, 800-CRAYOLA)

DESCRIPTION: Two kinds of crayons, especially designed for little hands, are easier to hold and harder to break than standard-size crayons. *So Big Crayons* (5″ × 9/16″) are for 2-year-olds who are beginning the basics of coloring. *Large Crayons* (4″ × 7/16″) are for 3- to 5-year-olds who are developing finer motor and eye–hand skills. They come with such palette-pleasing names as leap frog green, juicy orange, and firefly yellow.

COMMENTS: Crayon marks are washable and can be cleaned from most surfaces and clothing. The 16-piece *So Big Bucket* offers convenient cleanup and storage.

Crazy Combo (3–7, $15; Fisher-Price, 636 Gerard Ave., East Aurora, NY 14052, 800-432-5437)

DESCRIPTION: Is it a clarinet? Is it a sax? A trumpazoo? No, it's *Crazy Combo*—the musical building set. With 10 pieces that can be joined in a variety of ways, children can create real, and not so real, wind instruments. It also comes with a full-octave recorder, with instructions for fingering. And when the concert is over, everything can be neatly packed away in its own carrying case.

COMMENTS: *Crazy Combo* and other music makers in this section *(Rhythm Band, Tap-a-Tune, Tape Recorder)* are also suggested sensory playthings for special-needs kids.

Etch a Sketch (4 and up, $10; Ohio Art, One Toy St., Bryan, OH 43506, 419-636-3141)

DESCRIPTION: Turning the knobs on this "thirty-something" treasure causes lines, curves, and angles to appear on a screen, enabling children to form shapes, pictures, words, or whatever without pencils or markers. Erasing is easy, setting the stage for repeated do-overs.

COMMENTS: Quiet and self-contained, it keeps youngsters happily occupied during long trips.

Finger Paints (Redskin) (3 and up, $2.50; Milton Bradley, 443 Shaker Road, East Longmeadow, MA 01028-5247, 413-525-6411)

DESCRIPTION: No artistic ability is needed to savor the satisfying sensations of this self-expressive medium. Swirls and squiggles just seem to flow naturally from hand and arm movements. Kit comes with paints, glossy paper, spatula, and instructions.

COMMENTS: Painting of any sort is messy (which may be part of the fun). Aprons, old clothing, newspaper on the floor, and some supervision will paintproof both child and house. Youngsters should be involved in the cleanup process.

Magna Doodle (3 and up, $12.95; Tyco, 6000 Midlantic Drive, Mount Laurel, NJ 08054, 800-257-7728)

DESCRIPTION: In this very popular, no-battery, magnetic drawing toy, children can write directly on a screen using an attached pen and two design tools. The easy slide-bar eraser lets children start fresh whenever they want, providing countless chances for mistake-proof doodling, drawing, writing, and playing fun. Tracing, stenciling, spiral art, and other accessory sets are available for expanded and more structured activities.

COMMENTS: Small design tools need to be watched. *Magic Copier* (for ages 5 and up) lets kids print out their productions.

Rhythm Band Set (2–10, $29.50; Music for Little People, P.O. Box 1460, Redway, CA 95660, 800-346-4445)

DESCRIPTION: Strike up the band with this six-piece set containing a castanet, tambourine, triangle, jingle tap, block, and cymbals. An instructional rhythm book is also enclosed.

COMMENTS: All rhythm instruments (bells, rattles, cymbals, triangles, sand blocks, drums) are suitable for 2-year-olds. At 2½, horns and whistles become appropriate, and 3- to 5-year-olds can play other "blowing" instruments (harmonica, simple recorder), xylophone, and piano for one-finger tunes.

Soft Clay (3 and up, $3.99; Adica Pongo, Plattsburgh, NY 12901)

DESCRIPTION: Working with clay, one of those activities characteristic of childhood, enables young potters to pat, punch, poke, and pattern. As the name implies, unlike the regular self-hardening type, this kind remains soft without needing to be kept moist. *Play Doh* (Kenner), a claylike compound, can be used alone or with figures and designs for more directed experiences.

COMMENTS: While to younger preschoolers the process is more important than the final product, 4- and 5-year-olds will be more interested in modeling actual figures or objects. Although these and other listings in this section are nontoxic, children should be taught to keep all art materials out of their mouths.

Tap-a-Tune (2–6, $18–$27; Little Tikes, 2180 Barlow Road, Hudson, OH 44236, 800-321-0183)

DESCRIPTION: By matching colors on a keyboard with notes in a songbook, young pianists can play such tunes as *Mary Had a Little Lamb* and *London Bridge*. Or, perhaps, they'll prefer to just pound on the keys. No matter—either way they'll be learning about sounds and music.

COMMENTS: Real instruments—such as bells, drums, and tambourines—and wind-up music boxes are also prime choices for preschoolers.

Tape Recorder (3 and up, $40; Fisher-Price, 636 Gerard Ave., East Aurora, NY 14052, 800-432-5437)

DESCRIPTION: A tape recorder has always been a terrific toy choice. Not only does it provide hours of fun, it can spark singing, listening, and movement. Now a new feature, a hand-held microphone, makes it even better. Children can sing into the mike to accompany their tapes, or use it by itself to record their own made-up stories and songs. Easy-to-manage buttons permit preschool operation.

COMMENTS: *Easy Touch Tape Player* (Mattel) with a special safety "lock-out" feature lets parents control battery loading and volume. Both machines require batteries (not included) that must be kept out of children's hands because of danger of toxicity and choking. For recommended preschool recordings, consult chapter on audios.

FREE OR INEXPENSIVE MATERIALS

The following materials provide valuable information about play and playthings at little or no cost:

Cornell Cooperative Extension, Resource Center-GP, Cornell University, 7 Business and Technology Park, Ithaca, NY 14850.

Understanding Children through Play (321 REN 13M). Discusses fun with nature, science, books, music, rhythms, finger-plays, safety considerations, and homemade toys. $2.

National Association for the Education of Young Children (NAEYC), 1834 Connecticut Ave., N.W., Washington, DC 20009, 202-232-8777, 800-424-2460.

Helping Young Children Develop through Play: A Practical Guide for Parents, Caregivers, and Teachers (#345), J. K. Sawyers and C. S. Rogers. Suggests how adults can foster play with infants, toddlers, preschoolers, and school-agers. $5.

Play Is FUNdamental (#576), J. B. McCracken. Offers ways in which parents and caregivers can make play an enriching experience. Available in Spanish (#566). 50¢.

Toys: Tools for Learning (#571). Provides tips to help parents make wise toy choices for their children. Includes table of good toys and activities for children from birth through 8 years of age, a toy shopping checklist, and safety pointers. 50¢.

National Institute of Mental Health, Information Resources and Inquiries Branch, Office of Scientific Information, Room 15C-05, 5600 Fishers Lane, Rockville, MD 20857. Single copy is free.

The Importance of Play, Constance Stapleton and Herbert Yahraes. Contains information on toys and sex stereotyping, fantasy and imagination, how play helps development, and how parents can help.

The National Lekotek Center, 2100 Ridge Avenue, Evanston, IL 60201, 708-328-0001, Fax: 708-328-5514. $3.75.

Lekotek Play Guide for Children with Special Needs. Presents the importance of play, guidelines for toy selection, and advice on playthings suitable for children with various disabilities.

Preschool Publications, Inc., P.O. Box 1851, Garden City, NY 11530, 516-742-9557, Fax: 516-742-5007. $1.25 each.

Parent and Preschooler Newsletter. Three excellent back issues dealing with play and toys are "Guidelines to Help You Choose Toys for Your Preschooler," November 1990; "The Importance of Play in Your Child's Life," October 1987; "Choosing Good Toys for Your Preschooler," September 1986.

Toy Manufacturers of America, Toy Booklet, P.O. Box 866, Madison Square Station, New York, NY 10159-0866. Single copy is free; specify English or Spanish edition. Bulk orders may be ordered for a small fee.

The TMA Guide to Toys and Play. Highlights importance of play, parental involvement, safety, toy selection, labeling, and a guide to toys.

U.S. Consumer Product Safety Commission, Washington, DC 20207. Single copy is free.

Which Toy for Which Child, Birth through Age Five, Dr. Barbara Goodson and Dr. Martha Bronson. Covers children's abilities and interests, toy safety, and comprehensive guidelines for toy selection. Another booklet is available for children 6 through 12 years of age.

TOY CATALOGS

Catalogs provide an opportunity for parents and caregivers to become acquainted with a wide range of toys, save valuable shopping time, and protect against impulse purchases. However, with shipping costs and no in-store discounts, buying by catalog can be more expensive.

Many toy manufacturers sell only through distributors, not directly to the public, and, therefore, do not furnish catalogs. The companies listed below, however, will send one free upon request, although prices may be omitted. Those that contain playthings for special-needs children are indicated by the letter (S).

BRIO Scanditoy Corp., 6555 West Mill Road, Milwaukee, WI 53218-1240, 800-558-6863.

Childcraft, P.O. Box 29149, Mission, KS 66201-9149, 800-631-5657.

Constructive Playthings, 1227 E. 119th St., Grandview, MO 64030-1117, 800-255-6124.

Handicapped Children's Technological Services (S), P.O. Box 7, Foster, RI 02825, 401-861-3444.

Kapable Kids (S), P.O. Box 250, Bohemia, NY 11716, 800-356-1564.

Kaye Products (S), 535 Dimmocks Mill Road, Hillsborough, NC 27278, 919-732-6444.

LEGO Systems, P.O. Box 1138, Enfield, CT 06083-1138, 800-422-5346.

Little Tikes, 2180 Barlow Road, Hudson, OH 44236-0877, 800-321-0183.

Rifton/Community Playthings (S), Route 213, Rifton, NY 12471, 800-374-3866.

Texas Instruments, P.O. Box 53, Lubbock, TX 79408, 800-TI-CARES.

Today's Kids, P.O. Box 207, Booneville, AR 72927, 800-258-TOYS.

Toys for Special Children (S), 385 Warburton Avenue, Hastings-on-Hudson, NY 10706, 800-TEC-TOYS.

Toys to Grow On, P.O. Box 17, Long Beach, CA 90801, 800-874-4242.

Chapter 7

Videocassettes

The VCR has turned the TV set from a Pandora's box into the equivalent of an Aladdin's lamp,[1] and the children's video market is zooming. Both the volume and variety of kid-vid, as it is popularly known, are evidenced by the number of full-length movies, TV-related features, books on film, musical performances, cartoons, teaching tapes, and more. How does this affect the preschooler? Are videos just another form of passive entertainment encouraging young "video vegetables," or do they have some value?

VIRTUES OF VIDEOS

Videos can excite imagination, inspire thinking, invite interaction, expand interests, enhance learning—and they are wonderful electronic babysitters.

Videos offer:
- *Control.* Videos let families watch what they want when they want, providing a welcome alternative to, and freedom from, the power of commercial programming.
- *Expansion of literacy.* Videos, by linking film and books, can motivate and complement reading. Children can

watch old favorites or be introduced to future ones. Having the same or a related book handy, either before, during, or after viewing, further encourages the reading habit.

- *Medium for music.* Videos provide exposure to different types of rhythmic experiences that promote participation and response.
- *Opportunities for learning.* Videos help children to understand themselves, basic concepts, and the world around them.
- *Quality time.* They are also good vehicles for shared family fun.

VIDEO POINTERS

Libraries are ideal "starting-off" points in which to explore the world of video because they afford opportunities to sample many preselected, diverse videos at no cost. Taping appropriate television programs, such as specials or highly rated shows, are inexpensive ways to build a collection. Parents can enrich the viewing experience by discussing children's reactions and feelings to what they have seen. And, as with everything else, videos must be used in moderation and selected with care.

THE CHALLENGE OF CHOICE

Walking into the children's section of a video store, one can see rows of *Mutant Ninja Turtles* and *Masters of the Universe.* Parents often have misgivings about such a steady diet, but have probably exhausted all the Disney classics and have neither the time nor expertise to hunt up satisfactory substitutes. Since children gravitate toward videos of familiar TV characters (which are frequently just extensions of toy-inspired cartoons), parents better be ready with some suitable suggestions of their own.

THE BEST PRESCHOOL VIDEOCASSETTES

Here is a guide to wonderful, quality videos for children aged 2 through 5 (see "References" for more information). For convenience in finding a particular type, they have been grouped into categories of Storybook Favorites, Mostly Music, Memorable Movies, and Video Potpourri. Targeted ages are included as a general guide, but vary depending upon individual interests and abilities. Many titles can be found in libraries or stores, and, if interested in purchase, parents should try to do so from their local outlets to save shipping and handling charges. Titles can also often be obtained directly from the producer, although some prefer that they be ordered through distributors or local stores. A few videos that are out of print have been included because they are still available for rental. Sources of recommended catalogs with large selections are at the end of this chapter. Happy viewing!

Storybook Favorites

Babar the Elephant Comes to America (Ages 3–7, 30 minutes, $13.95, 1986, Children's Video Library, order through local store or catalog)

DESCRIPTION: The king of the elephants and wife Celeste sightsee in style on their visit to America. When they catch up with cousin Artur in Hollywood, they get a "star-tling" surprise in this "mammoth" movie narrated royally by Peter Ustinov.

COMMENTS: After seeing this video, children will probably enjoy returning to the original Jean de Brunhoff classic that started it all (see chapter on books).

The Cat in the Hat and Dr. Seuss on the Loose (Ages 3–7, 51 minutes, 1985, rental availability only, Playhouse/Fox Video)

DESCRIPTION: *The Sneetches* (about differences) and *The Zax* (about stubbornness) join the better known *Cat in the Hat* and *Green Eggs and Ham* in these all-Seuss, song-animated, sure-to-please stories.

COMMENTS: This version has been replaced by two separate cassettes ($9.95 each) which can be ordered through local stores. Be sure to have some Seuss books on hand for follow-up.

Corduroy and Other Bear Stories (3–7, 30 minutes, $19.95, 1984, Children's Circle, 800-KIDS-VID)

DESCRIPTION: This video links three little bears of storybook fame: *Corduroy,* a teddy who lost a button but found a friend anyway; *Panama,* a search for a dream land; and *Blueberries for Sal,* a maternal mix-up involving a young boy and a bear cub.

COMMENTS: These "un-bear-ably" good award-winning tales make one honey of a video.

Curious George (Volumes 1–3, 3–7, 30 minutes each, $14.95 each, 1983, Sony, 800-523-0823)

DESCRIPTION: Monkey business is the order of the day when inquisitive George visits all sorts of places (the ballet, zoo, library), does all sorts of things (fishes, skis, walks the pets), and gets into all sorts of trouble. Fortunately, the Man in the

Yellow Hat is always forgiving and always there to make things better.

COMMENTS: Each volume consists of six separate stories of five minutes each, which is good for short attention spans. An 83-minute video with more monkeyshines is also available.

Five Stories for the Very Young (2–6, 30 minutes, $14.95, 1983, Children's Circle, 800-KIDS-VID)

DESCRIPTION: A quintet of quintessential quality literature includes *Caps for Sale,* Esphyr Slobodkina; *Changes, Changes,* Pat Hutchins; *Drummer Hoff,* Barbara and Ed Emberley; *Harold's Fairy Tale,* Crockett Johnson; and *Whistle for Willie,* Ezra Jack Keats.

COMMENTS: A natural follow-up is *More Stories for the Very Young* with *The Little Red Hen, Max's Christmas, The Napping House, Not So Fast, Songolo,* and *Petunia.*

Happy Birthday, Moon and Other Stories (2–6, 30 minutes, $14.95, 1989, Children's Circle, 800-KIDS-VID)

DESCRIPTION: Five more favorites feature a birthday *(Happy Birthday, Moon),* new baby *(Peter's Chair),* rude awakening *(The Napping House),* wolf-outwitting *(The Three Little Pigs),* and an odd couple *(The Owl and the Pussycat).*

COMMENTS: Can be shown one story at a time or in combination depending on concentration capability.

The Maurice Sendak Library (3–7, 35 minutes, $14.95, 1989, Children's Circle, 800-KIDS-VID)

DESCRIPTION: A fine mix of Sendak fantasies *(Where the Wild Things Are, In the Night Kitchen)* and poems *(The Nutshell Kids* with *Chicken Soup with Rice, Pierre,* and two others) sung enchantingly by Carole King.

COMMENTS: A talk with the author, in which he reveals his childhood feelings, might be used as a springboard to explore emotions.

Sign-Me-a-Story (3 and up, 30 minutes, $14.95, 1987, Random House Home Video, 800-733-3000)

DESCRIPTION: Linda Bove, the talented, deaf Sesame Street actress, performs *Little Red Riding Hood* and *Goldilocks* using sign language, with accompanying narration and original music.

COMMENTS: Good for hearing-impaired children, this video also introduces children with normal hearing to another form of communication.

The Snowman (2–6, 26 minutes, $14.95, 1982, Sony, 800-523-0823)

DESCRIPTION: Every child's dream of a snowman coming to life is realized in Raymond Brigg's superb story. After visiting in the boy's house, it's off to the North Pole and Santa. Great visual sequences and exquisite orchestral score make this much-honored movie a treat for any time of year.

COMMENTS: Children can be encouraged to make up their own words to accompany both the wordless video and book.

Stories from the Black Tradition (3 and up, 52 minutes, $14.95, 1992, Children's Circle, 800-KIDS-VID)

DESCRIPTION: Five African-American Caldecott award winners are assembled in one outstanding tape. Includes *Why*

Mosquitoes Buzz in People's Ears, narrated by James Earl Jones, *Goggles, Mufaro's Beautiful Daughters,* and *A Story, a Story.*

COMMENTS: The beautifully illustrated books upon which these films are based should be close at hand before and after viewing.

The Velveteen Rabbit (4 and up, 30 minutes, $9.95, 1985, Random House Home Video, 800-733-3000)

DESCRIPTION: A boy's love brings a toy rabbit to life in this tender tale by Margery Williams touchingly told by Meryl Streep.

COMMENTS: This makes a wonderful read-aloud story, but preparation may be needed for some sad moments before the final happy ending.

Mostly Music

Baby Songs (1–4, 30 minutes, $14.98, 1987, Media Home Entertainment, 800-645-6600)

DESCRIPTION: The titles tell it all. With such names as "Share," "Security," and "My Mommy Comes Back," you know that this live-action, inventive video by Hap and Martha Palmer celebrates early challenges and concerns. A songbook is included.

COMMENTS: This extremely successful award winner was followed by *More Baby Songs, Even More Baby Songs,* and, for children aged 3–7, *Turn On the Music.*

Baby's Nursery Rhymes (1–5, 26 minutes, $14.98, 1990, Lightyear Entertainment, 800-229-STORY)

DESCRIPTION: Thirty-six traditional nursery rhymes updated with spirit and sparkle by Phylicia Rashad. Adapted from *The Baby's Lap Book* by Kay Chorao.

COMMENTS: Two others in this acclaimed *Stories to Remember* series are *Baby's Bedtime* (lullabies sung by Judy Collins) and *Baby's Storytime* (nursery tales performed by Arlo Guthrie).

Clifford's Sing-Along Adventure (3–6, 30 minutes, $19.95, 1986, Lorimar, order through local store or catalog)

DESCRIPTION: That beloved, big, red storybook dog takes kids on a fun-filled musical jaunt with imaginative renditions of familiar tunes.

COMMENTS: This colossal canine presents six *Fun with . . .* tapes that teach letters, numbers, sounds, shapes, rhymes, and opposites.

Disney's Sing-Along Songs (Various volumes, 2 and up, 28 minutes each, $12.99, Disney Home Video, 800-237-5751)

DESCRIPTION: Strike up the band for memorable melodies from the Disney collection. Each volume contains the scenes from the movies with on-screen lyrics. Particularly recommended in the series are *Under the Sea, Fun with Music,* and *Heigh Ho.*

COMMENTS: *Disney's Greatest Lullabies,* with such goodnight songs as "When You Wish upon a Star" from *Pinocchio* and "Dance of the Sugar Plum Fairies" from *Fantasia* can turn any child into a "Sleeping Beauty."

Elmo's Sing-Along Guessing Game (2–4, 30 minutes, $14.95, 1991, Random House Home Video, 800-733-3000)

DESCRIPTION: A terrific takeoff on TV quiz shows, in which video clues result in song-filled shenanigans.

COMMENTS: More super Sesame Street sing-alongs with *Sing, Hoot, and Howl,* an animal tribute, and *Sing Yourself Silly,* hilarious "moving" music.

Kidsongs: Music Video Stories (2–7, 25 minutes each, $11.99, 1987, Viewmaster/Tyco, 800-367-8926)

DESCRIPTION: The infectious Kidsongs Kids will get children singing along in no time to these time-tested tunes. Each video has live performances of 10 to 12 numbers with original musical arrangements. A lyrics songcard is included.

COMMENTS: Top titles in the series include *A Day at Old MacDonald's Farm; A Day with the Animals; Cars, Boats, Trains and Planes,* and *Very Silly Songs.*

Raffi in Concert with the Rise and Shine Band (2–5, 50 minutes, $19.95, 1988, A & M, 800-925-7272)

DESCRIPTION: This winning video gives children an opportunity to see as well as hear the remarkable Raffi. The more than 20 songs include some of his most popular, such as "Baby Beluga," "Shake My Sillies Out," and "Everything Grows."

COMMENTS: Also recommended is Raffi's first video, *A Young Children's Concert.* Consult the chapter on audios for blockbuster recordings that have sold in the millions.

Wee Sing Together (2–6, 60 minutes, $19.95, 1985, Price/Stern/Sloan, 800-421-0892)

DESCRIPTION: The popular Wee Sing series includes songbooks, audiocassettes, and music videos. On this tape, children sing-along, clap-along, and dance-along as they attend Sally's big birthday bash where toys and gifts come alive.

COMMENTS: Another celebration, *King Cole's Party,* is the backdrop for Wee Sing's *Nursery Rhymes.*

Memorable Movies

The Red Balloon (3 and up, 34 minutes, $14.95, 1956, Janus, order through local store or catalog)

DESCRIPTION: A poignant portrayal of a lonely French boy and the red balloon that follows him everywhere points up the magical powers of friendship and love.

COMMENTS: This wordless, sensitive multiaward winner will probably be appreciated more by older preschoolers. Due to the immense success of the movie, a picture book followed.

Walt Disney Cartoon Classics (2 and up, $12.99, widely available)

DESCRIPTION: Cartoons are almost synonymous with childhood. Donald, Mickey, Pluto, and Goofy are just some of the characters that have become part of our culture, and are available on cassettes for kids of all ages.

COMMENTS: These videos make good choices for family viewing.

Walt Disney Films (3 and up, various lengths, dates, and prices, Disney Home Video, 800-237-5751)

DESCRIPTION: Walt Disney, the master of animated entertainment, has left a legacy of magnificent movies. Most appropriate for younger children are *Alice in Wonderland,*★ *Bambi,*★

Dumbo, Lady and the Tramp, Mary Poppins,★ *101 Dalmatians, Peter Pan,*★ and *Pinocchio.* All are widely available (the ones followed by a star can be ordered through the toll-free telephone number).

COMMENTS: Although fantasies, these masterpieces contain universal feelings with which children (and adults, too) can empathize.

Winnie the Pooh and Tigger Too (3–7, 25 minutes, $12.99, 1974, Walt Disney, widely available)

DESCRIPTION: One of the best-known episodes in an animated series based on the A. A. Milne classic in which the overly exuberant Tigger's bouncing, trouncing, and flouncing drives everyone crazy.

COMMENTS: The lovable characters of Hundred-Acre Wood reappear in *Winnie the Pooh and: The Blustery Day, A Day for Eeyore,* and *The Honey Tree.*

Video Potpourri

The Animal Alphabet (2–6, 30 minutes, $16.95, 1985, Warner Home Video, order through local store or catalog)

DESCRIPTION: From alligator to zebra, children are introduced to animals and the alphabet in this double-header learning experience. The original songs that express each animal's rhythm and movement as well as each letter's sound are by Elizabeth Swados; the exceptional live-action film footage is by National Geographic.

COMMENTS: *Baby Animals Just Want to Have Fun* and *Meet Your Animal Friends* are also useful for teaching about animals, especially before or after a visit to the zoo.

Bill Cosby's Picture Pages, **Volumes 1–6** (2–6, 30 minutes each, 1987, currently out of print but available for rental)

DESCRIPTION: Incomparable Bill Cosby, assisted by Mortimer Ichabod Marker (a felt-tipped pen), helps kids master concepts of shapes, sounds, colors, numbers, letters, words, and thinking.

COMMENTS: The lessons are light and lively, and get a gold star from the National Education Association.

Don't Eat the Pictures: Sesame Street at the Metropolitan Museum of Art (3–9, 60 minutes, $14.95, 1987, Random House Home Video, 800-733-3000)

DESCRIPTION: Locked in a museum? Oh, no! Oh, yes! The Muppets can't get out, and take kids on a top-notch, tune-filled tour inspiring young art lovers everywhere.

COMMENTS: Although a bit on the old side for preschoolers, it can be used effectively to prepare for that next museum visit.

Jim Henson's Fraggle Rock (2–5, 30 minutes, 1986, rental availability only, HBO Video)

DESCRIPTION: This unforgettable, underground place of the long-time television series is filled with frolicking Muppets, Doozers, and Gorgs. As children enjoy the singing, dancing, and general good humor, they learn important lessons about getting along with others.

COMMENTS: The Muppets deliver the message that each one of us is special in *I'm Glad I'm Me.*

Lamb Chop's Sing-Along, Play-Along with Shari Lewis (2–5, 45 minutes, $14.95, 1988, Fries Home Video, 800-248-1113)

DESCRIPTION: Shari Lewis and her puppet friends, Lamb Chop, Hush Puppy, and Charlie Horse, are joined by a group of children in singing, dancing, clapping, rhyming, guessing, and playing games.

COMMENTS: Children at home will want to join in too, making this an inviting interactive video.

Learning about Numbers (2–5, 30 minutes, $14.95, 1986, Random House Home Video, 800-733-3000)

DESCRIPTION: Through music, animation, and comedy, the Count and his Sesame Street friends cleverly reinforce number recognition and counting to 20. An activity book is included.

COMMENTS: *Learning about Letters* is the alphabet counterpart.

Mister Rogers: When Parents Are Away (2–6, 66 minutes, $14.98, 1987, Playhouse/Fox Video, order through local store or catalog)

DESCRIPTION: Whether children are with a sitter or at day care, it's sometimes hard to be apart from those we love. Television's Mister Rogers, with song, straight talk, and neighborhood outings, helps children and adults deal with the stress of separation.

COMMENTS: *Music and Feelings* and *What about Love* also focus on feelings.

Richard Scarry's Best ABC Video Ever! (3–5, 30 minutes, $9.95, 1989, Random House Home Video, 800-733-3000)

DESCRIPTION: Huckle Cat, Lowly Worm, Bananas Gorilla, and their Busytown friends amble through the alphabet with a story for every letter.

COMMENTS: A companion *Best Counting Video Ever* takes kids on a scavenger hunt searching for objects to count from 1 to 20.

Romper Room Series (3–6, 31–40 minutes, $14.98, 1984, 1987, Playhouse/Fox Video, order through local store or catalog)

DESCRIPTION: This long-running nursery school show, with Miss Molly, Kimble, and the rest of the regulars, is now available at home for repeated replays often required for learning. Different tapes deal with animals, arts and crafts, movement and rhythm, the senses, and numbers, letters, and words.

COMMENTS: Produced in cooperation with the National Education Association, it contains tips for parents and related activities that can be shared.

Sesame Street Home Video Visits the Hospital (3–5, 30 minutes, $14.95, 1991, Random House Home Video, 800-733-3000)

DESCRIPTION: Poor Big Bird gets sick (even his feathers hurt) and he has to go to the hospital. We follow along as he learns how nice nurses and doctors really are, and that a hospital isn't such a scary place after all.

COMMENTS: A reassuring video that can prepare youngsters for a potentially frightening experience when they or someone they love becomes ill.

VIDEO CATALOGS

Catalogs provide opportunities to become acquainted with the wide variety of videos and to order hard-to-find titles. The companies below furnish catalogs free upon request and have toll-free telephone numbers for customer service and/or inquiries. Some also include listings of audiocassettes and books.

Children's Book and Music Center, 2500 Santa Monica Boulevard, Santa Monica, CA 90404, 800-443-1856, 213-829-0215, Fax: 213-820-0836.

Children's Circle, CC Studios, Inc., Weston, CT 06883, 800-KIDS-VID, 203-222-0002.

Educational Record Center, Building 400/Suite 400, 1575 Northside Drive, N.W., Atlanta, GA 30318-4298, 800-438-1637, 404-352-8282, Fax: 404-351-2544.

Kimbo Educational, P.O. Box 477, Long Branch, NJ 07740-0477, 800-631-2187, Fax: 908-870-3340.

Media Home Entertainment, 5959 Triumph Street, Commerce, CA 90040-1688, 800-645-6600.

Music for Little People, P.O. Box 1460, Redway, CA 95560, 800-346-4445.

Random House Home Video, 225 Park Avenue South, New York, NY 10003, 800-726-0600, 212-254-1600, Fax: 800-659-2436.

Upbeat, 163 Joralemon Street, Brooklyn, NY 11201, 800-872-3288, 718-522-5349.

Part II

THE BEST
RESOURCES
FOR ADULTS

Chapter 8

Books

There are many fine books that can help to make the important preschool years more productive, happier, and easier. The following books focus on child care and development, motivating literacy, and learning through play. They reflect the latest thinking of experts, hard-learned lessons from parents, and the most useful, reassuring information currently available.

CHILD CARE AND DEVELOPMENT

Ames, Louise Bates, and Frances Ilg. New York: Delta/Dell, $8.95 each.

Your Two-Year-Old: Terrible or Tender (149 pp., 1980)
Your Three-Year-Old: Friend or Enemy (168 pp., 1980)
Your Four-Year-Old: Wild and Wonderful (152 pp., 1989)
Your Five-Year-Old: Sunny and Serene (123 pp., 1981)
    This time-honored series focuses on each age, with its unique characteristics, routines, accomplishments, problems, and suggested toys and books.

Balter, Lawrence, with Anita Shreve. New York: Poseidon, 1987, 252 pp., $9.95.

Dr. Balter's Child Sense: Understanding and Handling the Common Problems of Infancy and Early Childhood
A famous child psychologist helps parents understand why children behave as they do and offers step-by-step techniques and solutions for dealing with today's specific child-rearing problems.

Brenner, Barbara. Bank Street School of Education. New York: Pantheon, 1990, 276 pp., $11.95.

The Preschool Handbook: Making the Most of Your Child's Education
Devoted to supporting and enriching the preschool experience, this handbook explains how to decide between home care versus preschool, choose a school, and deal with everyday routines and issues.

Caplan, Frank, and Theresa Caplan. New York: Bantam, 1984, 545 pp., $4.95.

The Early Childhood Years: The Two to Six Year Old
A minicourse on how children grow and learn that helps prepare for and avoid many of the common pitfalls during the critical preschool period.

Fraiberg, Selma. New York: Macmillan, 1981, 305 pp., $20.

The Magic Years
This million-copy best-seller, first published in 1959, focuses on understanding and handling problems of early childhood and probes personality development and behavior in warm, sensitive terms.

Galinsky, Ellen, and Judy David. New York: Ballantine, 1991, 504 pp., $20.

The Preschool Years
An anecdotal, immensely readable manual that applies problem-solving strategies that work to 100 issues that generally arise during the crucial 2- to 5-year-old period.

Gillis, Jack, and Mary Ellen Fise. New York: HarperCollins, 1990, 432 pp., $14.

The Childwise Catalogue
An invaluable guide, loaded with extensive, brand-specific recommendations of products and services that help consumers make intelligent and safe decisions for children from birth through age 5.

Goldstein, Robin, with Janet Gallant. New York: Penguin, 1990, 276 pp., $6.95.

Everyday Parenting: The First Five Years
A reassuring sourcebook that offers straightforward responses and no-nonsense suggestions to 90 most-often-asked parent questions.

Leach, Penelope. New York: Knopf, 1990, 553 pp., $18.95.

Your Baby and Child: From Birth to Age Five
Revised for the nineties, this child care and development favorite describes early feelings and needs at different stages, plus information on emergencies, first aid, safety, and illnesses.

Pomeranz, Virginia E., with Dodi Schultz. New York: St. Martin's, 1987, 260 pp., $3.99.

The First Five Years: The Relaxed Approach to Child Care
A doctor's down-to-earth, witty approach toward child rearing that advocates spending less time on routine tasks, and more on activities that really matter, like conversation, reading, playing, and cuddling.

Shelov, Steven P., and Robert E. Hannemann. American Academy of Pediatrics. New York: Bantam, 1991, 676 pp., $29.95.

Caring for Your Baby and Young Child: Birth to Age 5
A comprehensive reference from a distinguished organiza-

tion that combines both child-rearing and medical advice in one very complete volume. The first half deals with growth guidelines and parenting topics; the second half is an encyclopedic guide to health problems, common diseases, disabilities, and medications.

Smutney, Joan Franklin, Kathleen Veenker, and Stephen Veenker. New York: Ballantine, 1991, 224 pp., $8.95.

Your Gifted Child: How to Recognize and Develop the Special Talents in Your Child from Birth to Age Seven
A how-to book (fostering creativity, language, education, etc.) for parents of gifted children.

White, Burton L. Englewood Cliffs, NJ: Prentice-Hall, 1991, 380 pp., $10.95.

The First Three Years of Life
An in-depth classic guide to the mental, physical, social, and emotional development of infants and toddlers, overview of recent educational thinking, and real-world-tested advice on a wide spectrum of parenting issues.

MOTIVATING LITERACY

Cullinan, Bernice E. New York: Scholastic, 1992, 152 pp., $3.95.

Read to Me: Raising Kids Who Love to Read
A highly acclaimed reading specialist tells how to give children the lifelong treasure of reading with tips on when to start, how to use television wisely, how to make children readers and writers, plus a list of surefire read-aloud books for preschoolers to preteens.

Graves, Ruth, ed. Reading Is Fundamental. Garden City: Doubleday, 1987, 324 pp., $8.95.

The RIF Guide to Encouraging Young Readers
Hundreds of kid-tested activities, designed to engage kids from infancy through age 11 in the fun of reading, and an annotated list of more than 200 books.

Hearne, Betsy. New York: Delacorte-Delta, 1990, 228 pp., $9.95.

Choosing Books for Children: A Commonsense Guide
A prominent author and critic offers precise information on choosing appropriate books for children from preschool to young adults, today's best books, and more than 300 annotated selections.

Kimmel, Margaret Mary, and Elizabeth Segel. New York: Delacorte, 1988, 279 pp., $16.95.

For Reading Out Loud!: A Guide to Sharing Books with Children
A much-praised guide to making reading aloud a richly rewarding experience with 300+ suggested titles.

Lamme, Linda L. Washington, DC: Acropolis, 1985, 208 pp., $8.95.

Highlights for Children: Growing Up Reading
In a companion volume to *Growing Up Writing,* an early-childhood professor shares insights and activities for encouraging a love of reading from the very beginning.

Lipson, Eden Ross. New York: Times-Random House, 1991, 508 pp., $15.

The New York Times Parent's Guide to the Best Books for Children
Marvelous reviews of nearly 1,000 titles, organized into broad categories according to reading level from "Wordless Books" to "Young Adult," with numerous, helpful cross-references, by the children's book editor of the *New York Times.*

Oppenheim, Joanne, Barbara Brenner, and Betty D. Boegehold.
New York: Ballantine, 1986, 345 pp., $13.95.

*Choosing Books for Kids: How to Choose the Right Book for the Right
Child at the Right Time*
Superb in-depth studies of developmental stages from birth
through age 12, with implications and suggestions (more
than 1,500 titles) for suitable reading.

Rollock, Barbara. Hamden, CT: Garland, 1992, 200 pp., $35.

Black Authors and Illustrators of Children's Books
A second edition of a pioneering reference work that illu-
minates African-American contributors to literature with
biographies and bibliographies of 150 writers and artists.

Trelease, Jim. New York: Penguin, 1989, 290 pp., $9.95.

The New Read-Aloud Handbook
This enormously popular and influential handbook, now in
its fourth edition, focuses on the pleasures and importance
of reading aloud to children, how to coax kids away from
television, and a guide to more than 1,400 books.

PLAY AND LEARNING ACTIVITIES

Boehm, Helen. New York: Bantam, 1986, 161 pp., $8.95.

The Right Toys: A Guide to Selecting the Best Toys for Children
A great guide to more than 250 brand-name toys that en-
tertain and educate from infancy through school age, including sections for children with special needs and child
care professionals.

Braiman-Lipson, Judy, Deborah Fineblum Raub, and the editors
of Consumer Reports Books. Mount Vernon, NY: Consumers
Union, 1988, 282 pp., $7.

Toy Buying Guide
Compiled by safety experts, hundreds of toys are rated for play value, educational value, and durability based upon responses from more than 12,000 households.

Garvey, Catherine. Cambridge: Harvard University Press, 1990, 176 pp., $17.95; Paper, 1990, 184 pp., $7.95.

Play
An expanded, literate work that explores findings of recent research, relationships between play and social–cognitive development, play styles, and gender identity.

Hamilton, Leslie. New York: Crown, 1989, 173 pp., $9.

Child's Play: 200 Instant Crafts and Activities for Preschoolers
Crafts, games, and projects from very simple (newspaper hats and body tracings) to more complex (making and playing musical instruments, cooking and science experiments) for kids from 18 months to 6 years of age.

Jones, Claudia. Charlotte, NC: Williamson, 1988, 190 pp., $9.95.

Parents Are Teachers, Too: Enriching Your Child's First Six Years
Activities and ideas that turn everyday events into spontaneous learning experiences, and help parents and child share in learning fun.

Oppenheim, Joanne F. New York: Pantheon, 1987, 311 pp., $11.95.

Buy Me! Buy Me!: The Bank Street Guide to Choosing Toys for Children
A splendid resource for finding the best, most appropriate playthings for each age and stage from birth through age 11 with an evaluation checklist, toys to steer clear of, an overview of toyland, and a toy directory.

Rogers, Fred, and Barry Head. New York: Berkley, 1986, 251 pp., $7.95.

Mister Rogers' PlayBook: Insights and Activities for Parents and Children
TV's Mister Rogers presents more than 335 games and projects for self-expression, independence, curiosity, and character development.

Schulz, Linda, and Lisa Rappaport Morris. Champaign, IL: Human Kinetics, 1989, 232 pp., $13.95.

Creative Play Activities for Children with Disabilities
Designed to help infants to 8-year-olds with all types of disabilities grow through play, it details directions, benefits, equipment, and possible adaptations for 250 games and activities.

Segal, Marilyn, and Don Adcock. New York: Newmarket, 1986, 224 pp., $16.95; Paper, 219 pp., $10.95.

Your Child at Play: Three to Five Years
Inventive ideas for encouraging and enjoying the world of the preschooler divided into separate sections of conversational play, creative play, social play, and playing with letters and numbers.

Segal, Marilyn, and Don Adcock. New York: Newmarket, 1985, 193 pp., $10.95.

Your Child at Play: Two to Three Years
How 2-year-olds learn during play.

Chapter 9

Magazines, Journals, and Newsletters

This section contains a mix of publications for both parents and professionals with creative ideas, suggestions, and strategies to add spice and support to the preschool years. Reduced subscription rates are sometimes available, so it is a good idea to check before ordering.

Child. P.O. Box 3176, Harlan, IA 51593-0367, 800-777-0222.
A beautifully produced magazine with discerning articles by well-known writers, wide-ranging features (home, food, fashion, travel, health, media, and more), and reviews of products and services of what's new for kids ($15.94, 10 issues).

Day Care and Early Education. Human Sciences Press, 233 Spring Street, New York, NY 10013-1578, 800-221-9369.
Designed for child care professionals and early educators, this quality quarterly focuses on such relevant areas as learning, books, computers, health, special needs, staff development, and effective parent communication ($26).

Growing Child/Growing Parent. P.O. Box 620, Lafayette, IN 47902-0620, 800-388-2624.

> *Growing Child,* a unique parent newsletter that matches each monthly issue to the specific age of the child, describes growth and development from birth through age 6. The companion, *Growing Parent,* included free, addresses child-rearing concerns and issues ($14.95, 12 issues; sample available).

Ladies' Home Journal Parent's Digest. 100 Park Avenue, New York, NY 10017, 212-953-7070.

> Warm, witty advice from some of America's best-known authorities (one recent issue included Dr. Spock, Dr. Lawrence Balter, Dr. Burton White, Penelope Leach, and more) make this quarterly a multimedia compendium to raising children from birth through teens ($2.50 per issue).

The Oppenheim Toy Portfolio. 40 East 9th Street, New York, NY 10003.

> An unbiased, ad-free quarterly to the best (safe, fun, developmentally appropriate) toys, games, books, and videos for kids birth through 8, as well as those with special needs ($12).

Parent and Preschooler Newsletter. P.O. Box 1851, Garden City, NY 11530-0816, 516-742-9557.

> Each issue of this first-rate monthly for parents and professionals—filled with child development information, activities, strategies, recipes, and books for children and adults—explores a theme relevant to children from 1 to 6 years old ($25, 12 issues; special rates for school and English/Spanish editions).

Parenting. P.O. Box 56861, Boulder, CO 80322, 800-234-0847.

> An all-around publication geared to meeting the interests of

today's modern families with engrossing, informative articles that extend beyond the usual home and child care advice to include travel, sports, and finance ($18, 12 issues).

Parents' Choice. Box 185, Newton, MA 02168, 617-965-5913.
This distinguished quarterly reviews all aspects of children's media—books, television, movies, video, recordings, toys, software—even comics and rock'n'roll; its annual awards for the best children's products and experiences are highly trusted and respected ($18).

Parents Magazine. P.O. Box 3055, Harlan, IA 51593-4119, 800-727-3682.
A popular monthly with interesting articles and features on child development, health, education, food, fashion, beauty, money, work, and more. Although the magazine covers kids from crib through college, of special interest are the Read-Aloud Book and the "As They Grow" section, with columns on 2-, 3-, and 4-year-olds and 5- and 6-year-olds ($20, 12 issues).

Pre-K Today. P.O. Box 2075, Mahopac, NY 10541, 800-325-6149.
A practical periodical for teachers and caregivers that is loaded with ready-to-use activity plans for children 2 through 5, ideas for program development and parent communication, reviews of children's media, and much more ($29.95, 8 issues).

Totline. Warren Publishing House, P.O. Box 2250, Everett, WA 98203, 800-334-4769.
A bimonthly newsletter specifically geared to the 2- to 6-year-old, packed with open-ended art and language activities, simple craft and story ideas, sugarless snack recipes, songs, games, and teacher resources ($18, 6 issues; sample available).

Working Mother. P.O. Box 53841, Boulder, CO 80321-3841, 800-627-0690.

Targeted for the woman with a job outside the home, this value-priced monthly presents information helpful in both worlds, along with lots of time- and work-saving tips ($7.97, 12 issues).

Young Children. National Association for the Education of Young Children, 1834 Connecticut Ave., N.W., Washington, DC 20009-5786, 800-424-2460.

A bimonthly, professional journal of the NAEYC that presents scholarly but readable articles on expert classroom practices, research and theory, viewpoints on current issues, and book reviews for adults and children ($30, 6 issues).

Chapter 10

Professional Associations

The following nonprofit organizations work to advance the needs of children, parents, and professionals. They provide a wealth of information, services, and support, often at little or no cost; many maintain conveniently located local chapters throughout the country. These associations are valuable resources and are eager to help; one need not feel shy or hesitant about contacting them.

International Reading Association (IRA), 800 Barksdale Road, P.O. Box 8139, Newark, DE 19714-8139, 302-731-1600, Fax: 302-731-1057.

Devoted to improving reading instruction and promoting a lifetime reading habit. Provides professional development, research and support, and materials on reading and related topics for professionals and parents. Publications: bimonthly newspaper, *Reading Today;* four journals, *The Reading Teacher, Journal of Reading, Reading Research Quarterly,* and *Lectura y Vida.* Basic membership—$18.

Learning Disabilities Association of America (LDA), 4156 Library Road, Pittsburgh, PA 15234, 412-341-1515, Fax: 412-344-0224.
Dedicated to advancing the education and general welfare of children with learning disabilities. Provides advocacy, an information and referral service, and national resource center. Publications: bimonthly newsletter, *Newsbriefs;* semiannual journal, *Learning Disabilities.* Membership—$25.

National Association for the Education of Young Children (NAEYC), 1834 Connecticut Avenue, N.W., Washington, DC 20009-5786, 202-232-8777, 800-424-2460, Fax: 202-328-1846.
Works to improve the quality of services for young children from birth through age 8. Offers professional development, a national accreditation system for early childhood programs, information service, and public affairs activities. Publications: bimonthly journal, *Young Children.* Membership—varies depending upon type of membership and local affiliation.

National Association for Gifted Children (NAGC), 1155 15th Street, N.W., Washington, DC 20005, 202-785-4268.
Seeks to enhance educational opportunities for intellectually and creatively gifted youth through research and development, dissemination of information, and support of gifted programs. Publications: newsletter, *Communique;* journal, *Gifted Child Quarterly.* Membership—$45.

National Black Child Development Institute, Inc. (NBCDI), 1023 15th Street, N.W., Suite 600, Washington, DC 20005, 202-387-1281, Fax: 202-234-1738.
Focuses on child care, welfare, health, education, and improving the quality of life for African-American children. Monitors public policy and conducts public education, cultural heritage, and leadership programs. Publications: quar-

terlies *Black Child Advocate, Child Health Talk.* Membership—$25.

The National Lekotek Center, 2100 Ridge Avenue, Evanston, IL 60201, 800-366-PLAY, 708-328-0001, Fax: 708-328-5514.

Resource centers and play libraries throughout the United States that provide play counseling, home loan of toys, and family education to enhance the learning and enjoyment of children with disabilities. Individualized monthly training session—$10.

Reading Is Fundamental (RIF), 600 Maryland Avenue, S.W., Suite 500, Smithsonian Institution, Washington, DC 20024, 202-287-3371, Fax: 202-287-3196.

A reading motivation program to help youngsters from age 3 through high school discover the joy, and acquire the habit, of reading. Sponsors free book distributions in which children choose and keep their own selections, and publishes inexpensive parent brochures for encouraging young readers. Membership—free.

Southern Early Childhood Association (SECA), P.O. Box 5403, Brady Station, Little Rock, AR 72215, 501-663-0353, Fax: 501-225-8457.

Concerned with the well-being of young children and their families, SACUS offers professional development, resources, and public policy and training institutes. Publications: quarterly journal, *Dimensions;* position papers. Membership—through local affiliates; nonaffiliated membership—$15.

Chapter 11

Free or Inexpensive Materials

The following materials provide useful information on a wide variety of topics concerning preschool children either free of charge or at minimal cost. Some requests can be made via a toll-free telephone number; others require sending a business-size (#10, 9″ long by 4″ wide), self-addressed, stamped envelope. Availability and prices are frequently subject to change; some patience may be needed as delivery can take from 4 to 8 weeks.

PARENTING

Cornell Cooperative Extension, Resource Center-GP, Cornell University, 7 Business and Technology Park, Ithaca, NY 14850.

Choosing Child Care for Infants and Toddlers (321 HDFS 24), Polly Spedding. Advantages and disadvantages of in-home, family day, and center-based care, what to look for, and what questions to ask. $1; 6 pp.

Off to a Good Beginning: Getting Ready for Kindergarten (3221 HDFS 9), Patricia Ziegler. Qualities of good schools and effective teachers; suggestions for spring and summer planning. $1; 6 pp.

Terrific and Terrible Two-Year-Olds (321 HDFS 4), Jennifer Birck-mayer. Characteristics of, and how to deal with, this age group. $1; 4 pp.

The World of the Five-Year-Old (321 HDFS 17), Patricia Fender-Robinson. Language, perception, discipline, school, play, and imagination. $1; 6 pp.

3 and 4 Year Olds (321 HDFS 5), Gretchen McCord. Growth and characteristics of these ages. $1; 4 pp.

Understanding Children through Play (321 REN 13M), $2. See description in chapter on children's toys.

National Association for the Education of Young Children, 1834 Connecticut Avenue, N.W., Washington, DC 20009-5786, 202-232-8777, 800-424-2460. 50¢ each.

Beginner's Bibliography (#502), P. Greenberg, ed. An annotated list of recent and classic books, brochures, and periodicals for parents, teachers, and others who want to learn more about how young children grow and learn.

Finding the Best Care for Your Infant or Toddler (#518). Help for parents in making informed choices about care options for infants and toddlers. Ten-part foldout page.

Helping Children Learn Self-Control (#572). Basic techniques to help children develop self-discipline.

Love and Learn: Discipline for Young Children (#528). Positive approaches that work.

How to Choose a Good Early Childhood Program (#525). What to look for in a good program for children. Eight-part foldout page. Also available in Spanish (#510).

Play Is FUNdamental (#576). See chapter on children's toys. Also available in Spanish (#566).

So Many Goodbyes: Ways to Ease the Transition between Home and Groups for Young Children (#573). How families and teachers can work together to help children feel secure in their adjustment to a new child care or school arrangement.

Teaching Young Children to Resist Bias: What Parents Can Do (#565). Tips for parents and teachers to help children appreciate diversity and deal with others' biases.

Testing of Young Children: Concerns and Cautions (#582). Popularized version of NAEYC'S position on standardized testing of young children ages 3–8.

Toys: Tools for Learning (#571). See chapter on children's toys.

National Center for Missing and Exploited Children, 2101 Wilson Boulevard, Suite 550, Arlington, VA 22201, 800-843-5678. Free.

Just in Case You Are Considering Daycare. Finding quality providers, safety tips for children in day care, and detecting sexual abuse and exploitation. Eight-part foldout page.

Just in Case You Are Considering Family Separation. Suggested provisions for custody decrees, and steps to take to prevent or deal with parental kidnapping. Eight-part foldout page.

Just in Case You Need a Babysitter. Recommendations on finding and hiring a babysitter, and safety tips for children while parents are away. Eight-part foldout page.

National Institute of Mental Health, Information Resources and Inquiries Branch, Room 15C-05, Office of Scientific Information, 5600 Fishers Lane, Rockville, MD 20857, 301-443-4513. Single copies are free.

Charla Franca Como Tratar al Niño Enojado (SP 80-0781). Spanish publication on how to deal with the angry child, and constructive disciplinary strategies. 4 pp.

The Importance of Play (ADM 81-0969). See chapter on children's toys.

When Parents Divorce (ADM 81-1120). Issues, custody, reactions of children, new relationships. 22 pp.

National Organization of Mothers of Twins Clubs, P.O. Box 23188, Albuquerque, NM 87192-1188, 505-275-0955. Free.

Your Twins and You. Helpful hints to mothers of multiples. 8 pp.

The National PTA, 700 North Rush Street, Chicago, IL 60611-2571, 312-787-0977.

Children and Television: What Parents Can Do (B305). Viewing skills, television time, and effects of violence and advertising on children. Three-part foldout page. Single copies are free with #10, self-addressed, stamped envelope; 100 copies are $5.

Discipline: A Parent's Guide (B306). Helpful tips, setting and enforcing limits, and avoiding nagging and power struggles. Four-part foldout page. Single copies are free with self-addressed, stamped envelope; 100 copies are $10.

National Safety Council, Customer Service Department, 444 N. Michigan Avenue, Chicago, IL 60611, 312-527-4800, 800-621-7619. Single copies are free.

How to Find the Right Child Care Center (#52945-0000). Finding appropriate child care facilities, evaluating existing child care, such as staff qualifications, educational objectives, health and safety policies, staff/child ratios, meals, toys, and more. 16 pp.

Toy Manufacturers of America, P.O. Box 866, Madison Square Station, New York, NY 10159-0866. Single copies are free; specify English or Spanish edition.

The TMA Guide to Toys and Play. See chapter on children's toys.

U.S. Consumer Product Safety Commission, Washington, DC 20207. Free.

Which Toy for Which Child, Birth through Age Five. See chapter on children's toys.

LEARNING

American Federation of Teachers, 555 New Jersey Avenue, N.W., Washington, DC 20001, Att: Home Team, 800-526-0859. Free.

Home Team Learning Activities. More than 60 tips for turning everyday family activities into constructive learning experiences. Eight-part foldout page.

American Music Conference, 303 E. Wacker Drive, Suite 1214, Chicago, IL 60601. Single copies are free with self-addressed, stamped envelope.

Music and Your Child. See chapter on audios for description.

Apple Computer, Inc., 20330 Stevens Creek Boulevard, Mail Stop 36-AN, Cupertino, CA 95014, 800-776-2333. Single copies are free.

Macintosh Educational Software Guide. See chapter on computer software.

The Boston Globe, P.O. Box 2378, Boston, MA 02107-2378. Free.

The Young Reader. See chapter on children's books.

Center for the Study of Reading, 51 Gerty Drive, Champaign, IL 61820. Single copies are free.

10 Ways to Help Your Children Become Better Readers. See chapter on children's books.

The Children's Book Council, Order Center, 350 Scotland Road, Orange, NJ 07050-2398, 800-666-7608. Sample copies are free with #10, self-addressed, stamped envelope.

Choosing a Child's Book. See chapter on children's books.

Consumer Information Catalog, R. Woods, Consumer Information Center-Y, P.O. Box 100, Pueblo, CO 81002. 50¢ each; make checks payable to "Superintendent of Documents." See chapter on children's books for additional materials related to reading.

Help Your Child Do Better in School (450X). Tips for adults to help children improve study skills. 5 pp.

Help Your Child Learn Math (452X). Fun ideas to help young children connect their real-life experiences with the math they need to learn. 7 pp.

Cornell Cooperative Extension, Resource Center-GP, Cornell University, 7 Business and Technology Park, Ithaca, NY 14850.

An Alphabet of Activities for Preschoolers at Home (HDFS 35), Jennifer Birckmayer. Simple, fun-filled activities for parents and child providers to strengthen relationships and develop intellectual, physical, emotional, and social skills. $1; 4 pp.

International Reading Association, 800 Barksdale Road, P.O. Box 8139, Newark, DE 19714-8139, 800-336-7323.

Parent Booklets: A series of 16- to 24-page booklets that focuses on answering questions parents often ask about the education of their children. $1.75 each. See chapter on children's books for specific titles.

Parent Brochures: Practical concerns of parents and how they can help children develop reading skills and a lifetime reading habit. Single copies are free with #10, self-addressed, stamped envelope. See children's book chapter for additional titles related to reading.

Eating Well Can Help Your Child Learn Better

Your Home Is Your Child's First School (Also available in French and Spanish)

National Association for the Education of Young Children, 1834 Connecticut Avenue, N.W., Washington, DC 20009-5786, 202-232-8777, 800-424-2460.

> NAEYC's carefully researched and easy-to-understand brochures offer vital information on topics of interest. They are 50¢ each; 100 copies are $10. See chapter on children's books for description of titles related to reading.

More Than 1,2,3: The Real Basics of Mathematics (#575). Tips on making math an exciting part of children's lives.

National Institute of Mental Health, Information Resources and Inquiries Branch, Office of Scientific Information, Room 15C-05, 5600 Fishers Lane, Rockville, MD 20857, 301-443-4513. Free.

Learning While Growing: Cognitive Development. Language, understanding, memory, levels of thinking, conscience, and how parents can help. 14 pp.

The National PTA, 700 North Rush Street, Chicago, IL 60611-2571, 312-787-0977. Single copies are free with #10 self-addressed, stamped envelope; 100 copies are $10. Eight-part foldout pages.

Help Your Child Become a Good Reader (B323). See chapter on children's books.

Help Your Child Get the Most Out of Homework (B307). Advice on ways to improve homework skills.

Help Your Young Child Learn at Home (B309). Activities that make learning enjoyable and motivate and help children succeed in school.

Math Matters: Kids Are Counting on You (B313). Fun activities that help build math confidence and skills.

Reading Is Fundamental, Inc., Publications Department, 600 Maryland Avenue, S.W., Suite 500, Washington, DC 20024, 202-287-3220.

RIF has many booklets and brochures to help parents turn children on to reading. See descriptions in chapter on children's books.

HEALTH AND SAFETY

Aetna Life & Casualty, 151 Farmington Avenue, RWAC, Hartford, CT 06156, 203-273-2843. Single copies are free.

Bicycle Safety (AA-2055). Tips for bicycle care and safety. Six-part foldout page.

Keeping Danger Out of Reach: A Child Safety Guide (AA-3764). Precautions to take in and around the home to prevent accidents. 5 pp.

Play It Safe (AA-4356). Coloring book illustrating good child protection practices, and a burglary prevention checklist. 16 pp.

Save Your Child from Poisoning (AA-2162). Poisonous substances and plants, how to poison-proof a house, and what to do if someone is poisoned. Six-part foldout page.

Tuffy Talks about Medicine (AA-2286). Coloring book that teaches children never to take medicine by themselves or from anyone else. 14 pp.

American Academy of Pediatrics, Publications Department, P.O. Box 927, Elk Grove Village, IL 60009-0927. Single copy free with self-addressed, stamped envelope.

Choking Prevention and First Aid for Infants and Children (HE0066). Dangerous foods and items, prevention, and emergency procedures for infants under and over 1 year of age. Eight-part foldout page.

American Automobile Association (AAA), Safety Department, 1000 AAA Drive, Heathrow, FL 32746-5063.

Fragile . . . Transport Safely! (Stock #3400). A guide to child car safety seats from infants to children over 4. Sample copy free. Twelve-part foldout page.

Parents, Buying Your Child a Bike? (Stock #3207). Types of bicycles, fitting the bicycle to the child, and safety tips. Sample copy free. Eight-part foldout page.

Preschool Children in Traffic (Stock #3265). A series of four 15-page booklets plus a parent's guide to reducing accidents among children aged 3 to 6. $1.50.

American Dental Association, 211 East Chicago Avenue, Chicago, IL 60611-2678, 800-621-8099. Sample copies free.

The ABC's of Good Oral Health (W146). An alphabet coloring book that familiarizes kids with the dentist and good dental practices. 28 pp.

Dental Health Activity Book (W220). Coloring, drawing, dot-to-dots, and puzzles to teach good dental care. 24 pp.

Your Child's First Visit to the Dentist (W110). Why, when, and how often to take children to the dentist, and how to prepare for the visit. Two-part foldout page.

Your Child's Teeth (W177). Basic dental care and child development. 13 pp.

Closure Manufacturers Association, 1801 K Street, N.W., Suite 1105L, Washington, DC 20006. Free with #10, self-addressed, stamped envelope.

Tips on Child Safety. Advice on how to instill safety consciousness in preschoolers, and general home safety tips. Four-part foldout page.

Juvenile Products Manufacturers Association, Two Greentree Centre, Suite 225, P.O. Box 955, Marlton, NJ 08053. Free with #10, self-addressed, stamped envelope.

Be Sure It's Safe for Your Baby! Safety tips in the home and car. Twelve-part foldout page.

Metropolitan Life Insurance Company, Health and Safety Education Division, One Madison Avenue, New York, NY 10010-3690. Single copies free with #10, self-addressed, stamped envelope.

Child Safety. Health and safety hints for home and travel. 6 pp.
Immunization—When and Why. Recommended vaccines for children plus ways to keep the necessary records.
Personal Health Record. Provision for keeping medical records of immunizations, allergies, family history, etc.
Your Child's Health Care. Suggestions on how to find a doctor, community resources, and maintain optimum health.

National Association for the Education of Young Children, 1834 Connecticut Avenue, N.W., Washington, DC 20009-5786, 202-232-8777, 800-424-2460.

Merrily We Roll Along (#512). How to keep children busy while they are buckled up. 50¢.

National Center for Missing and Exploited Children, 2101 Wilson Boulevard, Suite 550, Arlington, VA 22201, 800-843-5678. Free.

Child Protection. Safety tips to help prevent child abduction and sexual exploitation. Also in Spanish: *Proteja a los Niños.* 8 pp.

National Society to Prevent Blindness, 500 East Remington Road, Schaumburg, IL 60173-4557, 708-843-2020, 800-221-3004. Sample copies free.

How's Your Vision? Family Home Eye Test (AB45). This do-it-yourself kit contains two sections—one for young children and another for other family members. The children's tests include the "E" game and an eye chart. The adult section contains glaucoma, distance, and near vision tests and an Amsler Grid test for age-related macular degeneration.

Play It Safe! (HB20). Basic safety tips to protect children from needless eye injuries. Eight-part foldout page.

Signs of Possible Eye Trouble in Children (CB10). Warning signs of vision difficulties. 2 pp.

Your Child's Sight (CB20). The development of vision, signs of eye problems, and types of treatment available. 12 pp.

New York State Division of Criminal Justice Services, Executive Park Tower, Stuyvesant Plaza, Albany, NY 12203-3764, 800-FIND-KID. Free.

How to Protect Your Child from Abduction by Strangers and What to Do if It Happens. Prevention, preparation, and education to avoid abduction. Eight-panel page.

U.S. Consumer Product Safety Commission, Washington, DC 20207. Free.

Emergency First Aid for Children. Alphabetized, quick-reference guide to help parents care for an injured child until professional help can be reached. Covers such topics as artificial respiration, bites/stings, bleeding, broken bones, burns/scalds, choking, convulsions, CPR, fainting, heat exhaustion, poisoning, and shock. Twelve-part foldout page.

Locked Up Poisons Prevent Tragedy. Ways to protect children against accidental poisoning. Six-part foldout page.

Poison Lookout Checklist. Potentially dangerous situations in the home that can lead to accidental poisoning. 2 pp.

YWCA of Flint, 310 East Third Street, Flint, Michigan 48502, 313-238-7621. 50¢. Spanish edition available.

You Belong to You. A coloring book for children 4 to 9 years old that seeks to reduce their vulnerability to victimization.

SPECIAL NEEDS

American Academy of Pediatrics, Publications Department, P.O. Box 927, Elk Grove Village, IL 60009-0927. Single copy free with self-addressed, stamped envelope.

Learning Disabilities and Children: What Parents Need to Know (HE0063). Definition, causes, common problems, warning signs, and identification of learning disabilities. Eight-part foldout page.

CIGA-GEIGY, 556 Morris Avenue, Summit, NJ 07901, Attn: Marketing Services, 800-631-1162. Free.

ADHD, Attention Deficit-Hyperactivity Disorder and Learning Disabilities, Larry B. Silver, M.D. Published in two forms—one for parents, and another for teachers—to aid in understanding and helping children with these disabilities.

Council for Exceptional Children, 1920 Association Drive, Reston, VA 22091-1589, 703-620-3660. Two-page fact sheets. Free.

Does Early Intervention Help? (Digest #E455). Reasons, cost effectiveness, and critical features of early intervention.

Early Intervention for Infants and Toddlers: A Team Effort (Digest #461). Public Law 99-457, services, and intervention team models.

Preschool Services for Children with Handicaps (Digest #450). The Individual Family Service Plan (IFSP), and types of available services.

Learning Disabilities Association of America, 4156 Library Road, Pittsburgh, PA 15234, 412-341-1515. Sample copy free.

Learning Disabilities—What Is It? A four-page informational pamphlet discussing definition, symptoms, dyslexia, social perceptions, behaviors, and treatment.

National Information Center for Children and Youth with Handicaps, P.O. Box 1492, Washington, DC 20013-1492, 800-999-5599. Free.

A Parent's Guide: Accessing Programs for Infants, Toddlers, and Preschoolers with Disabilities. Questions and answers about early intervention services for children from birth through 2 years old, special education services for children from 3 through 5 years old, and information about federal legislation. 20 pp.

National Institute of Child Health and Human Development, 9000 Rockville Pike, Building 31, Room 2A32, Bethesda, MD 20892, 301-496-5133. Free.

Developmental Dyslexia and Related Reading Disorders. Written for people with some background in the fields of reading and learning disabilities, this overview discusses scope of reading problems, symptoms, possible causes, teaching methods, and prognosis. 58 pp.

Facts about Childhood Hyperactivity. Diagnosis, causes, treatment, medication, psychological intervention, diet, research, and information sources for hyperactivity. 16 pp.

Facts about Dyslexia. Definition, symptoms, possible causes (educational, psychological, biological), treatment, prognosis, and research. 13 pp.

National Library Service for the Blind and Physically Handicapped, 1291 Taylor Street, N.W., Washington, DC 20542, 202-707-5100, Fax: 202-707-0712. Free.

Discoveries: Fiction for the Youngest Reader. Guide to selected books
available on disc, cassette, or in braille for preschoolers to
second graders. 71 pp.

*Parenting Preschoolers: Suggestions for Raising Young Blind and Visually
Impaired Children,* Kay Alicyn Ferrell, American Foundation
for the Blind. Information written to answer many parents'
questions about characteristics and schooling. 28 pp.

Kindergarten Readiness

Parents, realizing the importance of good beginnings, want their children's kindergarten experience to be as positive and successful as possible. It is natural, therefore, for them to wonder whether their youngsters are ready. World Book, Inc., conducted a survey to help identify what kinds of early learning experiences, skills, and knowledge kindergarten teachers felt kids needed to be prepared for school. They received over 3,000 responses, which they used to help formulate their Early World of Learning Program. The 105 desirable readiness skills that were identified are listed below.★

Size

Understands big and little
Understands long and short
Matches shapes or objects based on size

★Excerpted from *Getting Ready for School.* © 1987 World Book, Inc. Reprinted with permission of the publisher.

Colors and Shapes

Recognizes and names primary colors
Recognizes circles
Recognizes rectangles
Matches shapes or objects based on shape
Copies shapes

Numbers

Counts verbally through 10
Counts objects in one-to-one correspondence
Understands empty and full
Understands more and less

Reading Readiness

Remembers objects from a given picture
Knows what a letter is
Has been read to frequently
Has been read to daily
Looks at books or magazines
Recognizes some nursery rhymes
Identifies parts of the body
Identifies objects that have a functional use
Knows common farm and zoo animals
Pronounces own first name
Pronounces own last name
Expresses self verbally
Identifies other children by name
Tells the meaning of simple words
Repeats a sentence of six to eight words
Completes incomplete sentence with proper word

Has own books
Understands that print carries a message
Pretends to read
Uses left-to-right progression
Answers questions about a short story
Tells the meaning of words heard in a story
Looks at pictures and tells a story
Identifies own first name in manuscript
Prints own first name

Position and Direction

Understands up and down
Understands in and out
Understands front and back
Understands over (on) and under
Understands top, bottom, middle
Understands beside and next to
Understands hot and cold
Understands fast and slow

Time

Understands day and night
Understands age and birthday

Listening and Sequencing

Follows simple directions
Listens to a short story
Listens carefully
Recognizes common sounds
Repeats a sequence of sounds

Repeats a sequence of orally given numbers
Retells simple stories in sequence

Motor Skills

Is able to run
Is able to walk a straight line
Is able to jump
Is able to hop
Is able to alternate feet walking down stairs
Is able to march
Is able to stand on one foot 5 to 10 seconds
Is able to walk backwards for five feet
Is able to throw a ball
Pastes objects
Claps hands
Matches simple objects
Touches fingers together
Able to button
Builds with blocks
Completes simple puzzles (five pieces or less)
Draws and colors beyond a simple scribble
Able to zip
Controls pencil and crayon well
Cuts simple shapes
Handles scissors well
Able to copy simple shapes

Social-Emotional Development

Can be away from parents for two to three hours without
    being upset
Takes care of toilet needs independently

Feels good about self
Is not afraid to go to school
Cares for own belongings
Knows full name
Dresses self
Knows how to use a handkerchief or tissue
Knows own sex
Brushes teeth
Crosses a residential street safely
Asks to go to school
Knows parents' names
Knows home address
Knows home phone number
Enters into dinner-table conversation
Carries a plate of food
Maintains self-control
Gets along well with other children
Plays with other children
Recognizes authority
Shares with others
Talks easily
Likes teachers
Meets visitors without shyness
Puts away toys
Able to stay on a task
Able to work independently
Helps family with chores

Appendix

Toy Safety

The U.S. Consumer Product Safety Commission has set safety regulations for certain toys. Manufacturers must design and manufacture their products to meet these regulations so that hazardous products are not sold. In addition, many toy manufacturers also adhere to the toy industry's voluntary safety standards.

Mandatory Government Regulations

For All Ages:

- No shock or thermal hazards in electrical toys.
- Amount of lead in toy paint severely limited.
- No toxic materials in toys.

Under Age 3:

- Unbreakable—will withstand uses and abuses.
- No small parts or pieces which could become lodged in throat.
- Infant rattles large enough not to become lodged in throat and constructed so as not to separate into small pieces.

Under Age 8:

- No electrically operated toys with heating elements.
- No sharp points or edges on toys.

Industry Voluntary Standards for Toy Safety

- Puts age and safety labels on toys.
- Puts warning labels on crib gyms advising that they be removed from crib when babies can get up on hands and knees to prevent strangling.
- Assures that the lid of a toy chest will stay open in any position to which it is raised and not fall unexpectedly on a child.
- Makes strings on crib and playpen toys no longer than 12 inches so that cords cannot become wrapped around children's necks.

What a Parent Can Do

- Look for and read age and safety labels on toys.
- Explain and/or show the child how to use toys properly and safely.
- Keep toys intended for older children away from younger children who can be injured.
- Check all toys periodically for breakage and potential hazards. Damaged or dangerous toys should be repaired or thrown away immediately.
- Store toys safely. Teach children to put toys away so they are not tripping hazards, and check toy boxes and shelves for safety.

For further information, write to the U.S. Consumer Products Safety Commission, Washington, DC 20207, or call the toll-free hotline, 800-638-CPSC.

Notes

Introduction

1. Dolores Durkin, *Children Who Read Early* (New York: Teachers College, 1966).
2. Brian Cambourne, "Language Learning and Literacy," in *Towards a Reading-Writing Classroom,* eds. Andrea Butler and Jan Turbell (Portsmouth, NH: Heinemann, 1984).

Prologue

1. Ages 2 through 4 adapted from *How Does Your Child Grow and Learn? A Guide for Parents of Young Children* (Jefferson City: Missouri Department of Elementary and Secondary Education, 1988), pp. 4–5, 12–17.
2. *Getting Started in the All-Day Kindergarten* (New York: New York City Board of Education, 1983), pp. 1–2.
3. *Home Team Learning Activities* (Washington: American Federation of Teachers, 1988), p. 3.
4. Ibid.
5. Ibid., p. 2.

Chapter 1

1. David Lovald, as quoted in Michael Lev, "Children's Music Lures the Recording Giants," *New York Times,* 16 December 1991, p. D8.
2. Andrea Cascardi, *A Parent's Guide to Video and Audio Cassettes for Children* (New York: Warner, 1987), p. 81.
3. Ibid., back cover.
4. Jill Jarnow, *All Ears: How to Choose and Use Recorded Music for Children* (New York: Penguin, 1991), p. 18.

Chapter 2

1. Richard C. Anderson, Elfrieda H. Hiebert, Judith A. Scott, and Ian A. G. Wilkinson, *Becoming a Nation of Readers: The Report of the Commission on Reading* (Champaign-Urbana, IL: Center for the Study of Reading, 1985), p. 23.
2. Nancy Balaban, *Starting School: From Separation to Independence* (New York: Teachers College Press, 1985).

Chapter 4

1. Peggy Schmidt, "What Every Kid Needs to Know about Computers," *Child* (January–February 1990), p. 56.
2. Kevin J. Swick, *Appropriate Uses of Computers in the Early Childhood Curriculum* (Little Rock: Southern Early Childhood Association, 1989), p. 3.
3. Susan Pine, "A Basic Collection of Software for Children," *School Library Journal 37* (October 1991), p. 39.
4. Ellen Galinsky and Judy David, *The Preschool Years* (New York: Ballantine, 1988), p. 93.
5. Sandra Anselmo and R. Ann Zinck, "Computers for Young Children? Perhaps," *Young Children 42* (March 1987), p. 25.
6. Galinsky and David, p. 93.

7. Peter H. Lewis, "Software: Shopping at Home," *New York Times,* 3 November 1991, sec. 4A, p. 42.
8. Warren Buckleitner, "25 Top Children's Programs," *Compute 13* (December 1991), p. 11.

Chapter 5

1. "A New World of Kids' Magazines," *US News & World Report,* 20 August 1990, p. 66.
2. Joanne E. Bernstein and Mona Behan, "Good Reads," *Parenting,* June–July 1989, p. 63.
3. James L. Thomas, "Magazines to Use with Children in Preschool and Primary Grades," *Young Children 43* (November 1987), p. 46.
4. *Magazines and Family Reading* (Washington, DC: Reading Is Fundamental, 1988), p. 2.
5. Ibid., pp. 1–3.
6. Bernice E. Cullinan, "Children's Magazines: Fun and Informative," in *Magazines for Children,* ed. Donald R. Stoll (Glassboro, NJ: Educational Press Association of America; Newark, DE: International Reading Association, 1990), p. 8.
7. Thomas, p. 46.
8. *Magazines and Family Reading,* p. 5.

Chapter 7

1. Peggy Charren, "Shopping for Kideos," *V Magazine,* April–May 1989, p. 4.

Epilogue

1. *Getting Ready for School: What Kindergarten Teachers Would Like Your Child to Know* (Chicago: World Book, Inc., 1987), pp. 11–12.

References

Prologue: The Preschool Child

Getting Started in the All Day Kindergarten. New York: New York City Board of Education, 1983.

Home Team Learning Activities. Washington: American Federation of Teachers, 1988.

How Does Your Child Grow and Learn? A Guide for Parents of Young Children. Jefferson City: Missouri Department of Elementary and Secondary Education, 1988.

Chapter 1: Audio Recordings

Albrecht, Kay. "Enjoying Music Together." *Scholastic Pre-K Today,* Nov.–Dec. 1990, 63–65.

Andress, Barbara. *Music Experiences in Early Childhood.* New York: Holt, Rinehart & Winston, 1980.

Association for Library Services to Children. *Notable Children's Films and Videos, Filmstrips, and Recordings, 1973–1986.* Chicago: American Library Association, 1987.

Association for Library Services to Children. *Notable Films/Videos, Filmstrips and Recordings, 1987–1990.* Chicago: American Library Association.

Cascardi, Andrea E. *A Parent's Guide to Video and Audio Cassettes for Children*. New York: Warner, 1987.

Greenberg, Marvin. *Your Children Need Music: A Guide for Parents and Teachers of Young Children*. Englewood Cliffs, NJ: Prentice-Hall, 1979.

Jarnow, Jill. *All Ears: How to Choose and Use Recorded Music for Children*. New York: Penguin, 1991.

Parents' Choice Magazine. Waban, MA: Parents' Choice Foundation. Annual Awards Issues, 1987–1991.

School Library Journal. New York: A. Cahners/R. R. Bowker. Various issues.

Chapter 2: Books

Cullinan, Bernice E. *Literature and the Child*. 2nd ed. San Diego: Harcourt Brace Jovanovich, 1989.

Gillespie, John T., and Corinne J. Naden, eds. *Best Books for Children, Preschool through Grade 6*. 4th ed. New York: R. R. Bowker, 1990.

Graves, Ruth, ed. *The RIF Guide to Encouraging Young Readers*. Garden City, NY: Doubleday, 1987.

Greene, Ellin. *Read Me a Story: Books and Techniques for Reading Aloud and Storytelling*. Garden City, New York: Preschool Publications, 1992.

Hearne, Betsy. *Choosing Books for Children: A Commonsense Guide*. New York: Delacorte/Delta, 1990.

Huck, Charlotte E., Susan Hepler, and Janet Hickman. *Children's Literature in the Elementary School*. 4th ed. New York: Holt, Rinehart & Winston, 1987.

Kimmel, Margaret Mary, and Elizabeth Segel. *For Reading Out Loud!: A Guide to Sharing Books with Children*. New York: Delacorte, 1988.

Landsberg, Michele. *Reading for the Love of It: Best Books for Young Readers*. New York: Prentice Hall, 1987.

Lipson, Eden Ross. *The New York Times Parent's Guide to the Best Books for Children*. New York: Times/Random House, 1991.

Oppenheim, Joanne, Barbara Brenner, and Betty D. Boegehold. *Choosing Books for Kids: How to Choose the Right Book for the Right Child at the Right Time*. New York: Ballantine, 1986.

Trelease, Jim. *The New Read-Aloud Handbook.* New York: Penguin, 1989.

Chapter 4: Computer Software

Anselmso, Sandra, and R. Ann Zinck. "Computers for Young Children? Perhaps." *Young Children,* March 1987, 22–27.

Blank, Marion, and Laura Berlin. *The Parent's Guide to Educational Software.* Redmond, WA: Tempus-Microsoft, 1991.

Buckleitner, Warren. *Survey of Early Childhood Software.* Ypsilanti, MI: High Scope Press, 1991.

Buckleitner, Warren. "25 Top Children's Programs," *Compute,* Dec. 1991, 10–15.

Educational Products Information Institute. *The Latest and Best of TESS: The Educational Software Selector, 1991–1992 Edition.* Hampton Bays, NY: EPIE Institute, 1991.

Galinsky, Ellen, and Judy David. *The Preschool Years.* New York: Ballantine, 1988.

Lewis, Peter H. "Software: Shopping at Home," *New York Times,* 3 Nov. 1991, sec. 4A, 42–44.

Neill, Shirley Boess, and George W. Neill. *Only the Best, 1991: The Annual Guide to Highest-Rated Educational Software, Preschool–Grade 12.* New York: R. R. Bowker, 1990.

Neill, Shirley Boess, and George W. Neill. *Only the Best, 1990: The Annual Guide to Highest-Rated Educational Software, Preschool–Grade 12.* New York: R. R. Bowker, 1989.

Neill, Shirley Boess, and George W. Neill. *Only the Best, 1985–1989: The Cumulative Guide to Highest-Rated Educational Software, Preschool–Grade 12.* New York: R. R. Bowker, 1989.

Pine, Susan. "A Basic Collection of Software for Children," *School Library Journal,* Oct. 1991, 39–43.

Schmidt, Peggy. "What Every Kid Needs to Know about Computers," *Child,* Jan.–Feb. 1990, 56–58.

Swick, Kevin J. *Appropriate Uses of Computers in the Early Childhood Curriculum.* Little Rock: Southern Early Childhood Association, 1989.

Chapter 5: Magazines

Bernstein, Joanne E., and Mona Behan. "Good Reads." *Parenting*, June–July 1989, 63–66.

Estes-Rickner, Bettie, and Jeannie Johnson. "Periodicals in Elementary Schools." *School Library Media Quarterly 19* (1990), 53–56.

Katz, Bill, and Linda Sternberg Katz. *Magazines for Libraries.* 6th ed. New York: R. R. Bowker, 1989.

Magazines and Family Reading. Washington, DC: Reading Is Fundamental, 1988.

"A New World of Kids' Magazines." *US News & World Report*, 20 Aug. 1990, 66–67.

Parents' Choice Magazine, Waban, MA: Parents' Choice Foundation. Annual Awards Issues, 1987–1991.

Richardson, Selma K. *Magazines for Children: A Guide for Parents, Teachers, and Librarians.* 2nd ed. Chicago: American Library Association, 1991.

Stoll, Donald R., ed. *Magazines for Children.* Glassboro, NJ: Educational Press Association of America; Newark, DE: International Reading Association, 1990.

Thomas, James L. "Magazines to Use with Children in Preschool and Primary Grades." *Young Children*, Nov. 1987, 46–47.

Chapter 6: Toys and Games

Boehm, Helen, *The Right Toys: A Guide to Selecting the Best Toys for Children.* New York: Bantam, 1986.

Braiman-Lipson, Judy, Deborah Fineblum Raub, and the editors of Consumer Reports Books. *Toy Buying Guide.* Mount Vernon, NY: Consumers Union, 1988.

Oppenheim, Joanne. *Buy Me! Buy Me!: The Bank Street Guide to Choosing Toys for Children.* New York: Pantheon, 1987.

Oppenheim, Joanne. *Oppenheim Toy Portfolio.* New York: Oppenheim Toy Portfolio, Winter 1991–1992.

Parents' Choice Magazine. Waban, MA: Parents' Choice Foundation, Annual Awards Issues, 1987–1991.

U.S. Consumer Product Safety Commission. *Which Toy for Which Child, Ages Birth through Five.* Washington: U.S. Government Printing Office, 1988.

Chapter 7: Videocassettes

ACT Awards for Children's Home Video. Cambridge: Action for Children's Television, 1986–1991.

Cascardi, Andrea E. *A Parent's Guide to Video and Audio Cassettes for Children.* New York: Warner, 1987.

Charren, Peggy. "Shopping for Kideos," *V Magazine,* April–May 1989, 4.

Children's Video. New York: New York Public Library, 1988 and 1989.

Choosing the Best in Children's Videos. Videocassette. American Library Association, 1990.

Dewing, Martha, ed. *Children's Video Report.* Princeton, NJ. Various issues.

Green, Diana Huss, ed., and the editors of Consumer Reports Books. *Parents' Choice Magazine Guide to Videocassettes for Children.* Mount Vernon, NY: 1989.

Parents' Choice Magazine Annual Awards. Waban, MA: Parents' Choice Foundation, 1987–1991.

Regan, Lesley O., ed. *Media Review Digest.* Ann Arbor, MI: Pierian Press, 1990.

Schechter, Harold. *KIDVID: A Parents' Guide to Children's Videos.* New York: Pocket Books, 1986.

Epilogue: Kindergarten Readiness

Getting Ready for School: What Kindergarten Teachers Would Like Your Child to Know. Chicago: World Book, 1987.

ABOUT THE AUTHOR

 HARRIET FRIEDES, M.A., has many years of experience working with young children and their families as a teacher and a reading clinician. In addition, she is an educational evaluator for the New York City school system, president of an educational consulting company, a guest speaker at professional conferences, and the author of several books on education. Ms. Friedes is a resident of New York City.

Index

**Property of the Library
YORK COUNTY TECHNICAL COL
112 College Dr.
Wells, Maine 04090
(207) 646-9282**